# FLORIDA LORE

# FLORIDA LORE

*The Barefoot Mailman, Cowboy Bone Mizell,*
*the Tallahassee Witch and Other Tales*

## CAREN SCHNUR NEILE

THE
History
PRESS

Published by The History Press
Charleston, SC
www.historypress.net

*Front cover bottom, back cover top and bottom*: *Courtesy of Mark Stevens at postcardroundup.com.*
*Front cover, top middle*: Seminole Chief Osceola, by George Catlin. *Courtesy Wikimedia Commons.*
*Front cover, top left*: Al Capone. *Courtesy Wikimedia Commons.*

First published 2017

Manufactured in the United States

ISBN 9781467137829

Library of Congress Control Number: 2017953977

*For my first storytellers: my parents, Gloria Lees Schnur and Sidney J. Schnur, and my sister, Randi Jones*

# CONTENTS

# CONTENTS

CONTENTS

# ACKNOWLEDGEMENTS

My gratitude goes out to all those who accompanied me on the memorable journey that resulted in this book, especially my husband, Tom Neile. If you do not see your name below and know it belongs there, please note that like this research, I, too, am a work in progress. I sincerely appreciate you.

Carrie Sue Ayvar, Laurie Berlin, Todd Bothel, Tina Bucuvalas, Peggy Bulger, Mij Byram, Kaye Byrnes, Robert Carr, Cori Convertito, Winnie Edwards, Florida Humanities Council, Paul George, Susan Gillis, Carol Goad, Dave Gonzales, Lucia Gonzalez, Tamara Green, Amanda Hardeman, Amanda Irle, Susan Kirby, Kristin Lachterman, Liliane Nérette Louis, Lucrece Louisdhon-Lounis, Gary Mormino, Vanessa Navarro, Hilary Parrish, Bob Patterson, Tina Peak, Monica Drake Pearce, James Powell, John Shipley, Linda Spitzer, Brian Stoothoff, Ingrid Utech, Rodney Welch, Butch Wilson, Kuniko Yamamoto, Pedro Zepeda

# THE REAL FLORIDA

*My grandfather, Ben Buxton, was born in 1900. He grew up in a time when most of South Florida was rural and unsettled. His father and mother at one point lived close to present-day Fort Myers. One of the main industries in Southwest Florida at that time was commercial fishing. My grandfather and his brother, Jack, would mingle with some of the fishermen when they brought their catches to a local fish house.*

*One day, some of the fishermen were setting around the fish house swapping tales. One old man described an old, abandoned, two-story house that stood on a desolate stretch of beach. It had what was termed up north a "widow's walk," basically an area on the roof that had a porch around it. The homeowners could access this area to view the ocean and catch the cool evening breezes.*

*The old man described how on some nights a man could be seen walking along the upper-story porch of the abandoned home. This wasn't strange, but the fact that the man had no head was! My grandfather was intrigued with the story and sometime later elected to pay the home a night visit. He coerced his brother to accompany him on this trip. They both rode a mule, bareback, numerous miles before arriving at the lonely and forsaken homestead that faced the sea. The immediate yard was covered in shrubs, while a forest of pine and other trees infringed around the outer perimeters of the house. They dismounted and made their way silently to the edge of the woods, where they could clearly see the upper-story porch.*

Map of Florida. *National Atlas.*

*My grandfather and great-uncle waited patiently for several hours, but failed to see anything. Just before they decided to leave, a man emerged on the porch and stood facing the sea. They watched in awe, because the man had no head projecting from his shoulders. Jack had a cold and suddenly started coughing. My grandfather said the man turned and faced them. The sight terrorized both young men, who hurried quickly to the tethered mule. It is no surprise that my grandfather noted that the once slow-moving mule was driven through the night like a racehorse, as they headed for the safety of their home, miles away.*

*—Butch Wilson*

Welcome to the home of the headless man. Of the Wakulla Pocahontas, the snake that made Lake Okeechobee and the ghost of Bellamy Bridge. Welcome to the real Florida: a land of stories old and new, true and partly true and flat-out whoppers created long before—and long after—the land was acquired by the United States from Spain in 1821 and became the nation's twenty-seventh state nearly a quarter of a century later.

It has often been said that the explorer Juan Ponce de Leon came to Florida in the first place on the strength of a story, that of the Fountain of Youth. In fact, that belief is a story as well, invented by a political opponent for the purpose of discrediting the Spaniard years after his death. So with knowledge of a legacy like that, how can I suggest that such tales represent the "real" Florida?

As I write these words, I am surrounded by dozens of books by resident journalists and itinerant researchers and millions of digitized words from interviews, e-mails and other documents, all of which reflect a wide range of attitudes toward and reflections on this extraordinary place. Many of these observers of our state, the nation's first to be occupied by Europeans, lay claim to knowledge of, if not connection with, the "real" Florida. Some claim that the real Florida can be found only among the Seminole and Miccosukee peoples, representing the Creek, Timucua, Calusa and others who were supplanted, and mostly decimated, by European colonization. Others insist that the real Florida is found only among Cracker culture, reflecting those native-born Floridians boasting multiple generations of white ancestors with roots that are southern and, prior to that, Anglo and Celtic. Then there are those who say the term "real Florida" can solely be applied to those born in Florida, whatever his or her ethnicity, whose family has resided here a significant amount of time.

One thing that these definitions and their ilk have in common is their firm reliance on the facts on the ground. The history: native peoples lived here for at least twelve thousand years, and the Spanish landed in 1513. The geography: 8,462 miles of tidal coastline, more than thirty thousand lakes and that one-of-a-kind Everglades ecosystem. The climate: sub-tropical (north and center) and tropical (south). The population: 20.5 million. Then there is the industry. The foodways. The economics and demographics. In short, we are inundated with information.

Such facts are extremely important. And yet I am a storyteller, and we storytellers tend to have a slightly different idea of what is important. First off, we are interested at least as much in the unconscious—the playful, the desired and the feared—as in the measured and managed. Human beings, after all, are as right-brain irrational (or a-rational) as we are left-brain logical. One could argue that our emotions are as real as our observations. In fact, one could also argue that our emotions actually influence our observations.

Stories also comfort and connect because they kindle our emotions. When we hear a good story, we feel as though we were experiencing it for ourselves, that we are sharing an adventure with the teller. And thus we connect with both the teller and the other listeners. Psychologists have long noted that this emotional connection helps us remember a story more readily than we do disconnected, disparate facts or ideas.

What is more, the storyteller's stock-in-trade is oral narrative, with all its strengths and weaknesses. The strengths of oral narrative are obvious. Stories well told are the backbone of our religious beliefs for good reason, providing as they do structure and causality, and therefore meaning, to our seemingly random existence. A sense of meaninglessness, psychologists tell us, breeds depression.

Stories can also temporarily transport us, on the strength of our own imaginations, from a difficult present to a more sustainable past and, more to the point, future. This is why during the Great Depression, American moviegoers with little more than a few coins jingling in their pockets plunked a few of them down every week to take solace and gain hope in the storied lives of characters portrayed by such luminaries as Fred Astaire and Ginger Rogers and, through other media, in the life stories of the actors themselves. More recently, consumers worldwide have thrown down a few more coins for a television set and a computer—often in a home boasting few other amenities—to travel to, be entertained by and learn about the world in convenience and safety.

Which leads us to the great weakness of oral narrative. Yes, we feel as though we are experiencing a good story ourselves in real time, playing the scenes through our minds as we would those of a memory. But just as memory is selective, reflecting our own prejudices, when we hear a story, so, too, do we receive only what the teller chooses to convey. (There is certainly a narrative to history; in fact, there are many, and this is the challenge: we know that even historians disagree on how facts coalesce to form meaning.) Thus, we are more easily taken in by story than by other forms of rhetoric, which, incidentally, is why Plato exiled the poets—the playwrights and storytellers of his day—from his ideal Republic. He knew the power of narrative and its potential for persuasion and corruption, because he regularly employed it himself. He simply could not resist. And so we learn from Plato an important truth: storytelling is a neutral activity, to be used for good or ill. It is up to the listeners to harness their critical faculties to discern what is behind the story, and its teller, that has such potential to seduce. We also need to question the motives behind our own interpretations when we listen.

Case in point: one of the most pernicious Florida stories that spread like a virus throughout the state for many decades was the mistaken belief that the unique Everglades ecosystem was a wasteland, worthless swampland begging to be dried up and filled in and turned into something useful, like sugar cane fields or housing developments. As most Floridians now recognize, the environmental cost of this dangerous story has been incalculable.

Another important example of the persuasive power of narrative resides in the contrasting "black" and "white" legends surrounding Spain's colonization of the New World. These legends get to the very foundation of the demographic clash that characterizes the state's history. At the start of the sixteenth century, Father Bartholeme de Las Casas, a Spanish historian, social activist and Dominican friar, helped to perpetuate the idea that Spain's treatment of colonial indigenous peoples was inhumane. Slaughter and slavery, he claimed, led to the destruction of not only native peoples in the New World but also their religion and culture. The concept became known as the Black Legend, or *La Leyenda Negra*. Although the country's treatment of the natives was certainly often brutal, many historians argue that it was no worse than that of other nations, but that Spain, by virtue of its enormous influence on the world stage, was singled out for denunciation.

In the mid-twentieth century, Spain retaliated against the defamatory Black Legend with its own "White Legend," arguing that the country had greatly benefited the natives by, among other things, introducing them to Christianity, thereby putting an end to human sacrifice. Spain further claimed that colonization had proved a boon to the indigenous tribes by introducing them to modern tools and other resources. The two narratives are alternate interpretations of the same set of events, shining a vital light on, as well as making a serious critique of, the entire narrative project.

Then there is the question of memory. Yes, we remember better when we hear a story, but memory is rarely if ever perfect. We color the details of stories with our own experiences and prejudices each time we retell them. This real-life game of "telephone" keeps cultural traditions vibrant and relevant. But it plays havoc with the concept of authenticity.

*And yet.* Florida has a rich history of traditional narrative, dating back millennia, to a time when its indigenous peoples listened to and learned from their tribal storytellers. What mattered then (and I suggest still matter now) were truths that were far deeper and richer than those of yesterday's archives or today's news feeds. The oral narrative tradition, with its tendency toward both intentional and accidental improvisation, worked rather well for a long time. It was the development of commerce, relying as it does on the precise recollection of numbers, dates and documentation, that necessitated written language and the verifiability it engendered.

## DIVERSE FLORIDA FOLK

This collection of stories celebrates Florida folk, in all their diversity: what people who live in the state think and feel and imagine, as much as what they see and hear and do and where they come from—in short, who and what they are. And so, to identify the real Florida, we must first determine who are the Florida folk.

First, the easy part of the answer: according to folklorists, every stratum of society is included among the "folk," rich or poor, young or old, PhD or pre-K. Our cultural traditions predate and precede education or class; they are available to and from us all. What is more, virtually every school child knows that long before transatlantic flight, globalization and the Internet, the United States was already a study in variety, welcoming tired and poor teeming masses from the time of its inception and long before.

When Ponce de Leon, former governor of Puerto Rico, arrived on the Atlantic coast, he called the spot—which he thought was an island—*La Florida*, in honor of the feast of *flores* (flowers) celebrated at Easter, which coincided with his landing. At the time, up to twenty-five thousand indigenous people resided in the area. As the Spanish population grew, the native numbers quickly and disastrously diminished due to war, slavery and illness. And as the need for manual labor grew, increasing numbers of slaves were abducted and imported, both from the Caribbean and from Africa. Voluntary or not, new residents came from all over the world in great numbers, and they still do. At this writing, as many as one-fifth of Florida residents are foreign-born, with three-quarters of these from Latin America. No wonder more than two hundred languages are spoken in the homes of the state's public school students.

Hand in hand with cultural diversity, this state has enjoyed, and been challenged by, extraordinary growth. While in 1830 the official population was just under 35,000, that number increased by more than 50 percent in the next decade, and the pattern continued into the beginning of the twentieth century. By 1950, Florida residents numbered more than 2.5 million, and ten years later, the population jumped nearly 80 percent, to just about 5 million. It has more than quadrupled since then—giving rise to bumper stickers that proudly proclaim car owners "Florida Natives."

As a result of this influx of new Floridians, native communities of Seminole and Miccosukee share borders with Crackers, Africans, French, English, Greeks, Cubans, Haitians, Jamaicans, Puerto Ricans, Nicaraguans, Hondurans, Colombians, Mexicans, Jews, Japanese and others—all of whom are here as a result of their own or someone else's pursuit of a better life, and all of whom have brought with them their stories, both those that are frequently shared and those long-buried.

Make no mistake—Florida's diversity and growth are not points to be taken lightly. Around folk festivals, conference rooms and kitchen tables, lovers of Florida and traditional culture have hotly debated this point. What lore, people ask, deserves the distinction "Florida"? Following the lead of scholars in the field, including that of the current and former Florida State folklorists, I choose to answer the question simply: that which is transmitted informally and held dear by those who self-identify as Floridians. However exotic they may appear, these are the traditions that underlie the behavior, decisions and beliefs of our fellow residents. We need to know them if we are to know our neighbors. We need to know our neighbors if we are to know ourselves.

This is not a new attitude, initiated by twenty-first-century political correctness. According to folklorist Martha Nelson in Tina Bucuvalas's *Florida Folklife Reader*, the founders of the Florida Folk Festival were aware of the importance of inclusiveness since the festival's inception:

> *At the first festival in May 1953, Czechoslovakian dance and embroidery, Angelo fiddling, French Huguenot storytelling, Minorcan Easter rituals, shape-note singing, children's rhymes, African American folk tales, turpentine camps songs, and the lore of Cow Creek Indians were interspersed with stylized music club and academic renditions of British ballads and southern beliefs....On Sunday morning the program of sacred music included Mormon, Jewish, Greek, Danish, African American, and Primitive Baptist singers, as well as one performance on the musical saw.*

Clearly, the festival founders understood that Florida folklore includes the traditions of all Floridians.

# FOLK NARRATIVE, FLORIDA-STYLE

If the storytellers and the stories that are told in and about Florida are first and foremost a study in variety, it is also important to note that there is something in folklore in general, and folk narrative in particular, that embraces unity. That is not to say it is nativist, however. Far from it. Archetypes, tale types and motifs are fancy terms for the basic patterns and building blocks that serve to unite the folk narratives of all cultures. Through strangely similar, if at times seemingly quite different, tales of mass destruction and resurrection, of tricksters and heroes and hauntings, we humans share a powerful bond: universal frames through which we make sense of our shared human experience. They are paradigms that are constantly shifting, yet always approximate each other at their core.

First, a quick definition: the term *folklore* refers to cultural products and traditions (narrative, dress, dance, food, art, music, games, etc.) that share three primary characteristics: (1) they are transmitted vertically (between generations) and horizontally (across generations); (2) this transmission occurs by informal means (predominantly orally and, more recently, via the Internet); and (3) each transmitter (informant) puts his or her personal stamp on the material. (A fourth criterion, that the material is of unknown authorship, is a bit more controversial. While no one person claims the copyright for hopscotch, for example, some of the oeuvre of Bob Dylan is considered to belong to the genre of folk music, in large part because it is in the style of those earlier, often anonymous, products. In addition, orally transmitted personal and family experience stories, or memorate, are also considered examples of folk narrative.)

Scholars have provided two general explanations for the fact that similar cultural products exist across borders and cultures. The first: conquerors, travelers and merchants spread stories like seeds on their journeys throughout the world. The second: these patterns comprise the human collective unconscious—that is, they are forms that are part and parcel of our human makeup, virtually embedded in our DNA. The truth is likely an amalgam of the two theories; in any event, the result is the same. Thus, while a tale called "Cinderella" may exist in only a few western cultures, "Cendrillon," "Yeh-Shen," "Rhodopis" and "Vasilisa" are stories of the same general tale type told in, respectively, France, China, Egypt and Russia. Although we may not find glass slippers in all of these stories, we do find a young person, in these cases female, who rises in status by the end of the tale.

## Folk Narrative

So this book is a collection of stories, but not just any stories. The life's work of an individual is not generally the stock-in-trade of folklorists. The only reference to that great former Florida resident Ernest Hemingway you will find in these pages, for example, is as a character. Instead, I focus on retelling stories originally passed down orally as folktales, legends, myths and urban legends. Folktales, represented here by stories such as "Epaminondas," are purely fictional tales, the original purpose of which was primarily entertainment but also socialization. Legends, including the story of Juan Ortiz, are based on fact—a real-life person, place or situation—but sprinkled with a generous helping of creativity. Myths, such as that of "Amaterasu the Sun Goddess," contrary to the colloquial use of the term to mean *falsehood*, are sacred stories often told at specific seasons or times of the day and said to contain the deepest truths of the human experience: the universal building blocks of our dreams and our nightmares. And speaking of nightmares, urban legends (i.e., "The Skunk Ape") provide chills and, often, a glimpse into our conscious or unconscious fears of mechanization and modernity.

## The Sections

I have divided the text into four sections. In "Fish, Fishermen and Other Peculiar Critters," I examine stories of non-human creatures and the human creatures who engage them, particularly those with a connection to water. This section contains a wide range of tales, from the real-life "legendary" (as in, the stuff of legend) fisherman Jesse Linzy to the Seminole story of how a snake created the real Lake Okeechobee. The second section, "Ghosts, Witches and Other Unsettling Stuff," dealing as it does with the supernatural and unsettling, also contains a mix of genres. Whether or not you believe that Robert the Doll possesses strange supernatural powers, for instance, the illusion of Spook Hill is simply strange, but very real.

"Legends and Legendary Folks" focuses on famous places and people and the stories, some mostly true and some mostly questionable, of people and places well known to Floridians in days gone by and, in some instances, up to the present. And finally, in "The Wide World of Florida Storytelling," we meet some of our diverse Florida storytellers and the myths and folktales that reflect their backgrounds.

## "TRUTHINESS"

And so we find ourselves back where we started. In an era replete with "truthiness" (a term popularized by the comedic news anchor Stephen Colbert), fake news and even fake*lore*—which refers to cultural products that pass for traditional but that are, in fact, commercially or individually produced, such as Mason Locke Weems's tale of George Washington and the cherry tree or Seminole alligator wresting—one might well ask how I dare assert that the fictional or fictionalized stories of a place represent its true nature. Why spread rumors and flat-out lies? Don't we have enough trouble discerning fact from fiction already? Are not journalism and history simply more useful, if not also more important?

The easiest answer to that question is that purveyors of history, news or folk narrative all bear the responsibility of telling their audiences which genre they are presenting and where their material came from, and audiences bear the responsibility to demand that information. (If someone tells us what she thinks or what she wants us to think, we have reason to be wary, but we may not know how to question her truth until we do our own research. Similarly, if a good storyteller tells us a good story, she takes us on a journey after which, ideally, she allows us to reach our own conclusions. The best storytelling asks questions rather than provides answers.)

When Orson Welles appeared on the radio on Halloween night in 1938 with "fake news" of a Martian invasion (the famed "War of the Worlds"), it was on a popular broadcast called *Mercury Theatre on the Air* that featured literary works. There were continuous interruptions to assure listeners that they were listening to a fictional show and not a real newscast. Some people panicked, but it could be argued that this was hardly the fault of the artists or broadcasters. *Caveat emptor*. Buyer, or in this case listener, beware.

I offer a slightly more complicated answer to the question of truthiness with respect to Florida, however. In popular imagination, Florida emerged early on as paradise on earth, replete with gorgeous weather and spectacular ocean views. Equally well known, of course, it has more recently been characterized as the sun-kissed state of dark Ponzi schemes and still darker boiler rooms, swampland for sale to unsuspecting Yankees, criminal careers destroyed by Old Sparky the Electric Chair and political careers destroyed by hanging chads and the hilariously lewd oeuvre of journalist and novelist Carl Hiassen—who swears he "does not have to make stuff up"—and an earlier and considerably more nefarious Carl, the so-called Count Carl von Cosel (aka Carl Tanzler), who lived seven years with the corpse of his beloved. So here I am collecting a book's worth of Florida folktales and legends, the kooky, unverifiable underbelly of a state with verifiable (some might say *certifiable*) documented characters that are already trending in the direction of kooky! Again, why bother with "loony" folk narrative when we have so many loony folk?

Here are three more good reasons:

*Folk narrative matters.* Because folk narrative is familiar on a visceral, if sometimes unconscious, level, it is a perfect way to introduce non-Floridians and new residents alike to the state and its people. Folk narrative demonstrates not just knowledge and history but also the group's unconscious—its most playful pranks and its darkest dreams. To paraphrase storyteller Jim May, "Myths are the dreams of the community; dreams are the myths of the individual," a philosophy that reflects the theory, mentioned above, of the collective unconscious, the wellspring of wisdom common to all humankind.

If folklore, specifically the types of folk narrative we will examine here, did not speak to the very core of the human experience, why would it be continuously transmitted from generation to generation, like Grandma's silver, or from friend to friend, like a Christmas fruitcake? (I am not suggesting that we always *enjoy* the stories, mind you, just that they fulfill some deep function.) By definition, folk narrative prevails, and it does so because it is effective. It effectively entertains, enlightens, inspires, reflects experience or emotion and/or fulfills some other need or desire in the individual and the community. This means that when we encounter folk narrative, we gain a deeper understanding of a culture's experience of reality—even if the stories themselves are not always based in reality. We storytellers have a saying: "Everything that I tell you didn't necessarily happen, but everything I tell you is true." Again, the nature of that truth is a matter for philosophers and sages, not journalists.

*Folk narrative should be preserved.* If folk narrative matters, then as a storyteller and lover of culture, I want to keep these tales alive. Now you may be thinking: hold on; you just explained that the stories have lasted this long because they fulfill an important function! Why must you work to keep them alive? And that's a good point. My answer is, in this moment in history, human beings are inundated—overwhelmed, one might say—with stories not only of all kinds and from all sides. We are living in a time when "the story" is king, whether because we have so many ways to tell our own stories by means of technology or because we are bombarded with so many voices and are trying to make sense, or meaning, of what we hear. Stories from storytelling corporations like Disney and story-selling companies like Nike and Tom's. Stories from personal experience such as those featured on stage, on radio and on the Internet. Stories from politicians and from news sites. Who is to say that folktales and legends will make it to the front of a line containing tell-all memoirs and titillating reality shows? An argument could be made, I suppose, for an evolutionary perspective: survival of the fittest material. But some material speaks with a louder voice or carries a bigger stick. Just because some voices fail to drown out others does not necessarily mean that they deserve to be ignored.

The impetus to keep the tales alive, incidentally, is why this book contains, as often as possible, stories that I have retold in such a way that the reader can retell them, too. You may choose to make some adjustments, depending on your personality, interests and audience. Professional storytellers typically collect as many variants, or versions, of a tale as possible, retain what the variants have in common (think of a Venn diagram: whatever overlap there is among the versions is most likely the most authentic material, and thus worth keeping) and then infuse their own personalities and imagination, employing their unique language and details, so that the story comes alive. I encourage you to embark upon the same exercise.

*Most Floridians come from elsewhere.* I am also writing this book for personal reasons. I am among the 65 percent or so of Florida residents who were not born in the state—the second-largest non-native U.S. state population, by the way, behind Nevada. I did not grow up with these stories, nor did I come of age with the fascinating people and places that spawned them. Discovering them as an adult, I was charmed and more than a little cowed by the sheer volume and breadth of the material. I fell in love with Florida by leaving my little enclave (both physically and through listening and reading) and exploring the beauty, depth and knowledge of my adopted home. If I had not been a storyteller, I might have done that another way. But for me, this method of getting-to-know-you makes the most sense. At my most fortunate, I have been able to both travel and enjoy the stories, such as driving to Ormond Beach and seeing Tomokie's statue, experiencing the phenomenon of Spook Hill in Lake Wales or visiting the Clewiston Inn and the Seminole Inn in Indiantown.

In contrast, a good many of my university students are Florida natives. They are sometimes annoyed, or perhaps just cannot see the point, when I tell them that the Walt Disney Company's variants of time-honored and time-tested folktales represent at least as much a corporate agenda as a cultural one. I am often unable to explain to their satisfaction why those who share stories by word of mouth or over the Internet are in a better position to express what the people believe than is an $85 billion publicly held company.

Actually, they are right to be perplexed. In their discussion of schema theory, Claudia Strauss and Naomi Quinn describe a cultural feedback loop that works something like this: we see Disney movies because they satisfy something in us, but they satisfy something in us because we have been programmed by seeing them in the first place. So which came first, the Disney chicken or the cultural egg?

Of course, anything that derives from humankind is, by definition, *socially constructed*. That is to say, the versions of stories developed by corporations are in one way human creations every bit as much as those passed down mouth to mouth (or, more recently, computer to computer). An important difference is in their origin and their goals. The non-corporate human urge to spread a story, or a tradition, or a recipe, can come from something as simple as excitement, delight, fear or belief, without an interest in whether the story will generate income or persuade others to behave in a certain way. Yes, individuals from punishing parents to public speakers at times use stories to fulfill an agenda, including, incidentally, the Brothers Grimm. But there are so many other incentives for sharing them, as well, such as something as simple as: "You're not going to believe what I just heard...."

One more point about our Orlando neighbors: Disney has helped keep folk narrative alive, albeit in a form that is, in my view sadly, more often than not considered definitive. I hope this book performs the first of these functions without falling into the pitfall of the second. Read these stories. Swim around in them. And retell them. They are ours. They are us.

## *Sources*

George, Paul. In-person conversation, January 7, 2017.

Hardeman, Amanda. Telephone conversation, December 24, 2016.

Nelson, Martha. "Nativism and Cracker Revival at the Florida Folk Festival." In *The Florida Folklife Reader*, edited by Tina Bucuvalas. Jackson: University Press of Mississippi, 2012.

Strauss, Claudia, and Naomi Quinn. *A Cognitive Theory of Cultural Meaning*. Cambridge, UK: Cambridge University Press, 1997.

Wilson, Butch. Personal e-mail correspondence, December 8, 2016.

# PART I

# FISH, FISHERMEN AND OTHER PECULIAR CRITTERS

The term "fish tale" refers not only to a story about swimming creatures with gills and fins but also to the kind of tall tale that gets bigger and more unlikely with every telling—much like the size of that marlin your cousin caught last summer.

What is it about the water that engenders such flights of fancy? Maybe it's the fact that we humans live on land, and thus the sea is a place of mystery and imagination. Maybe it's that it's dark under water, and far from civilization, and wilder, potentially, than Key West at Mardi Gras. Or maybe it's just because things down there can be just—so—strange.

## ERNEST HEMINGWAY THE FISHERMAN: A LEGENDARY KEY WEST RESIDENT

According to Dave Gonzales, the director of the Hemingway House in Key West, the legendary author Ernest Hemingway made it his business to perpetuate the tales of wine, women and wild living that surrounded him during his lifetime and have existed ever since. Hemingway—who was born in Illinois in 1899 and died sixty-two years later in Idaho—and then-wife Pauline Pfeiffer maintained a permanent residence at 907 Whitehead Street throughout the 1930s. In fact, the author wrote several of his best-known works while living in the Keys. When he wasn't writing, he was often found

When not writing, Hemingway fished in the Keys. *Lloyd Arnold, Wikimedia Commons.*

engaging in deep-sea sport fishing, particularly in pursuit of giant tuna and marlin. Hemingway also fished in the Marquesas Keys and Dry Tortugas, along with Bimini and the Gulf Stream off the coast of Cuba.

Apparently, the author was enjoying a fishing trip with his friends, affectionately known as the "Mob," at one of the Dry Tortuga islands when a fierce tropical storm stranded the group for weeks. According to one story, Hemingway met his eventual first mate Gregorio Fuentes during that period.

Gonzales explains that like real mobsters such as Machine Gun Jack McGurn, "Papa" Hemingway fished with a gun. Unlike McGurn, however, he used his machine gun solely to shoot the sharks that were trying to "apple-core," or nosh on, the prize-winning tuna he had on his line. That is to say, he was not trying to pulverize the catch itself.

And speaking of critters, cats also occupy a significant role in the Keys Hemingway legend. Today, forty or fifty felines, many of which sport six toes on their front paws and some an extra one in the back as well, reside in and around the former residence. The story goes that a sea captain who befriended Hemingway presented him with his own six-toed cat after the author admired it. Supposedly, that first cat's name was Snow White, but since then, with few exceptions, Snow White's progeny have all been named for celebrities.

## FLORIDA'S SEA (AND LAKE) MONSTERS

Some uncanny-looking Florida sea life is not the stuff of urban legends at all. Take the notorious "green monster," which erupts periodically in the St. Johns River. Everyone in the area knows the term refers not to a modern-day Godzilla but, rather, to noxious green algae. (A different form of marine algae is responsible for the dreaded red tide on the Gulf coast.)

But some sightings are more aptly described as close encounters of the cryptid kind—that is, animals that do not adhere to biologists' classification systems and are believed by most of them simply not to exist.

The same St. Johns River, for example, has been the site of several sea monster sightings, most notably in the late 1950s and early '60s. A thirty-foot serpent in Lake Clinch was sighted in Polk County at least as early as the turn of the twentieth century, while Pensacola, Jacksonville Beach and the New River Inlet in Broward County have had their own sea creature scares. Then there is the monstrous critter that attacked the divers off the Gulf coast; the Lake Worth Lagoon Monster, which also goes by the name Muck Monster; and the Lake Tarpon Monster, known as Tarpie to his friends. Tarpie is said to be about twenty feet long in his stocking fins.

Perhaps the most famous Florida sea monster, and certainly the oldest, hails from the area around St. Augustine. In November 1896, two boys came

Florida's sea monsters come in a variety of shapes and sizes. *New York Public Library Digital Archives.*

upon a strange carcass of about twenty-five feet in length, complete with tentacles and a jagged tail, in the waters off Anastasia Island. It is said to be one of the earliest examples of a globster, or organic blob.

In nearly every case, the creature looks about the same: a brontosaurus-like body with dark, rough skin, with or without horns and with a human face. Just so you know.

## HOGZILLA

Who knew that the love children of domestic pigs and wild boars roam free throughout the South? One might question whether this is the stuff of fact or fantasy, but some of the nation's most credible sources have paid attention. The National Geographic Channel reported in a special broadcast that an eight-hundred-pound creature was brought down in Georgia in 2004. And *The Hunt for Hogzilla* was a TV movie made in 2014 about a five-hundred-plus-pound specimen residing in North Carolina.

With feral hogs in every county, Florida has its share of Hogzilla and Hog Kong sightings, as well. One of these monsters supposedly weighed in at over half a ton and measured twelve feet in length. A recent entry in the annals of big pigs, Hog Kong, reportedly a massive 1,140 pounds, was shot in rural Okahumpka, southwest of Leesburg, by a .44 magnum. Said his killer, "I didn't realize he was that big, or I would have gotten a different gun."

Then there's the red-eyed Ghost Hog, which seems to appear and disappear at will around the Panhandle, east of the Apalachicola River.

Is it all a bunch of hogwash? You be the judge.

# THE BIRTH OF LAKE OKEECHOBEE:
## A SEMINOLE STORY

It should come as no surprise that a lake as large and important as Okeechobee would have its share of legends attached to it. The name means "big water" in the indigenous language Hitchiti, and they weren't kidding. At more than 730 square miles or about half a million acres, Lake Okeechobee is the second-largest freshwater lake in the United States—so big that it actually affects the weather. Located north of Everglades National Park and south of Orlando, it supplies water not only to the unique ecosystem but also, directly and indirectly, to 6.5 million residents along Florida's east coast.

At one time, the six-thousand-year-old Okeechobee was known as *Laguna del Esperitu Santo*, or Lagoon of the Holy Spirit. That mystical element may or may not have something to do with the oddities surrounding the lake. Scads of human skulls and other bones, which may be one hundred or one thousand years old, have been found in the shallows. Then there is the "Curse of the Everglades Triangle," which is supposed to explain the 1972 Eastern Airlines crash (101 fatalities) and the ValuJet crash (110 fatalities) in 1996.

Lake Okeechobee may or may not have been created by a giant snake. *USDA.*

And then there is the following Seminole tale. The beloved native teller Betty Mae Jumper, who included the story in her collection *Legends of the Seminoles*, sets it at the lake, but not at its birth. Another variant by Peg Brown, based on Jumper's tale, and a third version by Creek/Cherokee storyteller Jackalene Crow Hiendlmayr take us further back to reveal a surprising origin story. Spoiler alert: it involves an extremely large snake. Here is my retelling.

There were once two brothers who lived with their parents and their tribe in the swampland wilderness known today as the Everglades. These boys were known throughout the area as such successful hunters that they never returned empty-handed. And so it often fell to them to go out and find food for their people.

One day, the two went out on a hunt as usual, but this time, to their surprise and disappointment, they found no deer, no birds, no turtles, no nothing. They wandered farther and farther from home, determined not to fail in their duty to their people.

When night fell, the boys found a hollowed-out tree trunk they could just fit into together in order to catch some much-needed sleep.

During the night and unbeknownst to them, the rain crashed down in torrents. In the morning, the younger one awoke, desperate for breakfast. He didn't have to go far before he saw two enormous bass jumping around on the wet grass. He didn't know what they were doing there, but he didn't ask questions. He let his stomach do the thinking for him. He had already started a fire and begun to cook the fish when his big brother appeared.

"Those fish don't look right," the older boy said. No "good morning, how did you sleep," or anything else.

"What are you talking about?" said his brother. "They're fish, aren't they? Besides, aren't you hungry? I know I am!"

"Our mother said never to eat something that looks weird, and there's something weird about them. The color's all wrong. Besides, they're too big. Too fat. Too *something*."

The other boy laughed. "Too big? Too fat? Next you'll be telling me they're too delicious! Suit yourself; I'll eat them both."

And so he did. And when he was finished, he made sure to lick every finger, for good measure. Twice.

The two boys put out the fire and continued on their way. They hadn't gone far, however, when the younger brother, now walking single file a little behind the other, suddenly stopped.

"Hey!" he cried out. "Wait! Something's wrong!"

The older boy turned and approached him. "What's the—what the—?" To his horror, his little brother's arms and legs were beginning to fuse together into one tube-like appendage. As the two stared down, his skin grew scaly and hard.

"I—I think I'm turning into a snake!" he screamed. "Go get the elders! Go get the family! Go as quick as you can and get help!"

By the time his brother returned with his people, all that was left of the young man were his terrified dark eyes. The rest of him had become an enormous snake at least thirty feet in length. When the villagers had gathered around it, the snake raised his head and, in the young man's voice, began to speak.

"I have neglected the ways of my people," he said. "I should never have eaten something that didn't look right. I knew better. My mother taught me better." As the crowd watched in shock, he added, "I am lost to you now as a person, but let my punishment be a lesson to all of you not to abandon our traditions."

Then the enormous snake began to whirl and whirl around itself in a bigger and bigger circle, and the weight of its body sank it farther and farther into the wet earth. As it circled, the heavy rains began again, filling the hole it had made with its movements. When the others could no longer see it, the snake shot away to the north, making a deep furrow that almost immediately filled with rainwater.

It is said that the hole created by the snake's body became Lake Okeechobee, and the furrow is the Kissimmee River.

## BIG MAN JESSE LINZY: A PONCE INLET FISHING LEGEND

Even today, a man who looked like Jesse Linzy would raise eyebrows. At six feet, eight inches tall, he was the only guide massive enough and muscular enough to row his boat out of Mosquito (now Ponce) Inlet against the tide. He was so strong that he could hoist over his shoulders a couple of one-hundred-pound bags of cement without batting an eye, and his feet were so big that he had to cut out the tops of the largest shoes he could find to let his toes stick out.

At the turn of the twentieth century, Jesse Linzy was an African American fishing guide extraordinaire in the little town just north of New Smyrna

Jesse Linzy with his catch. *Ponce de Leon Inlet Lighthouse Preservation Association.*

Beach—at a time when many rich white men in the South did not take kindly to spending the day with, and taking instruction from, someone who didn't possess the same color skin.

Born in Savannah, Georgia, in 1872, the man who became known as the "giant of Ponce Park" arrived in Mosquito Inlet about 1909, took a job as a handyman and was promptly told to construct a sidewalk leading from the lighthouse to the river. (That walkway is so sturdy, it's still in use a century later.) Bartola Pacetti, who had owned and subsequently sold the land on which the lighthouse stood, used the cash from the sale to build a hotel nearby. Having seen Linzy's work firsthand, he hired him on.

Linzy, who was rarely seen off the job without a fishing pole in his hand, was soon besieged with questions about the best places to fish. When he mentioned this to his boss, Pacetti saw a golden opportunity to help out his employee, his guests and himself, all at the same time. He soon transformed his employee into a professional fishing guide. Linzy made sure his clients did well—as long as they showed up on time. Otherwise, he wouldn't bother leaving his hammock.

Eventually, Jesse Linzy became such a fixture at the Pacetti Hotel that even when a former guest bought the place, she kept him on, along with his wife, Miss Ida. And when the big man died in 1955, his obituary contained the following words: "He was affectionately known not only as the Mayor but also as the giant of Ponce Park. He was also known from north to south as the best fisherman along the Florida coast."

## MOB FISHING IN FORT LAUDERDALE

Game fishing captain Jimmy Vreeland spent much of his time in the 1920s and '30s ferrying celebrities around South Florida's New River and out to sea. Thus, when a group of well-dressed Chicagoans hired him to take them shark fishing, he was only too happy to oblige, and they set off in his thirty-five-footer, *Agnes*. The men didn't have much patience for the sport, however. After an hour of hand-to-mouth combat with a two-hundred-pound specimen, the leader, Vito, said, "Fuhgettaboutit," and politely inquired of the captain if he could use his .45 pistol.

Operating on the theory that the customer is always right, Vreeland shrugged. Each man then proceeded to reach for his holstered gun. The fishing picked up immediately. It took about five minutes for them to shoot four sharks, weighing up to four hundred pounds apiece. The tourists demurred on the standard offer to take their pictures with their catch, and Vito subsequently handed Vreeland a twenty-dollar bill to keep his mouth shut.

Lucky for us, he didn't. The captain later learned that Vito was, in fact, "Machine Gun" Jack McGurn, aka Vincenzo Antonio Gibaldi, the Capone associate most famously connected with the St. Valentine's Day Massacre and the 1927 maiming of the singer and comedian Joe E. Lewis in Chicago.

Vreeland didn't have to wait long to spill the beans, either. McGurn was fatally shot the day after Valentine's Day in 1936.

## OLD HITLER: A SHARK'S TALE

Considering the length of the Florida coastline along both the Atlantic Ocean and Gulf of Mexico, it's no surprise that a monster shark figures prominently in state lore. If anything, it's surprising there aren't more. The subject of Florida's most famous shark tale is so prominent that it even had a featured role on a Discovery Channel special during the cable giant's Shark Week.

For all the media hoopla, however, Boca Grande historian Johns Knight Jr. claims that *he* is, in fact, the source of the legend of the twenty-foot hammerhead shark known as Old Hitler. According to Knight, back in 1968, he and two imaginative friends pulled together bits and pieces of shark tales they'd heard over the years for their school paper, and—long before the phrase was in use—the story went viral.

Who knows? So many anglers have come forward with eyewitness accounts of hair-raising encounters, one can only wonder which came first: the sightings or the stories about them. Real or not, why is the shark called Old Hitler? The answer may be more interesting than you imagine.

The following story is a composite of all those I have learned:

Boca Grande Pass is a narrow strip of water connecting Lee and Charlotte Counties at the mouths of the Peace and Myakka Rivers, along Florida's Gulf coast. It is one of the deepest natural inlets in the state, with ledges that make perfect underwater sanctuaries for all manner of extraordinary, and extraordinarily large, marine life. The area has become world famous both for tarpon-fishing humans and for tarpon- and mullet-eating sharks.

Joe had been catching mullet off and on in those waters since he was a boy. Only the war had been able to put a hold—albeit temporary—on his fishing exploits. During World War II, German U-boats preyed heavily on shipping in the Gulf. While dirigible blimps patrolled the shore, nervous merchant mariners and supply vessels began to report strange blobs floating in the sea. At least some of these were believed to be not enemy vessels but rather hammerhead sharks, a particularly large and aggressive member of the species. Joe had heard about them for years, but he had never gotten a close enough look to be sure he had encountered one.

One fine summer morning in the early '60s, he set out on his old fifteen-footer, hoping for a good catch. The fish had been biting well that week, and he was feeling optimistic. Life, he reflected, was good.

Sure enough, by the end of the day, Joe's net was full and his belly empty. He was just about to pack it in when he spotted over his shoulder a dark-colored fin in the distance, making its way steadily toward him. He froze. Then he saw the distinctive flat, mallet-shaped head. The thing was as big as a pickup truck. And it was headed straight for his stern.

He watched in horror as the shark drew steadily closer. And then, as it lurched up out of the water toward his net full of fish, Joe got another shock. This shark was bigger than his boat and covered with scars. In all his years on the water, he had never seen anything like it.

He was scared, but he was more mad than scared. He'd worked hard from sun-up to sundown and was not about to give over his entire catch to some pea-brained fish. Not daring to take his eye off the creature for a moment, he reached back for the machete he always carried on board. The cleaver-like knife had fulfilled a wide range of purposes over the years, but this would be its last task. He took careful aim and flipped the heavy steel blade into the air. It landed with a soft "plunk," square in the dorsal fin of the monster.

The mighty fish dove straight down, and Joe hoped he had seen the last of it. But then it took one last mighty leap in the air. With a sharp intake of breath, he saw the full effect of his blow. Bizarrely, the wound was in the shape of a swastika. There was no doubt. It was a symbol he knew all too well from the war.

With a shiver, he turned the boat toward home.

## THE ENDANGERED SKUNK APE

The strangest thing about the Florida Skunk Ape is not that it is known by so many names—Florida Bigfoot. Louisiana Bigfoot. Bardin Booger. Swamp Ape. Stink Ape. Swamp Cabbage Man. Myakka Ape. Swampsquatch.

The strangest thing is not that it is said to resemble a six- or seven-foot-tall shaggy human, weighing upward of four hundred pounds, or to walk upright on two legs (with four toes on each foot) at speeds of as much as twenty-two miles per hour, or to spend a great deal of its time hanging out in trees, or to possess eyes that glow in the dark, or even to smell positively putrid.

Since the early 1950s, there have been thousands of real, imagined or invented sightings of Florida's so-called Skunk Ape, mainly in the Everglades but also in the Keys and in Bardin, less than an hour's drive from Gainesville, in the north of the state. Folks have claimed to have taken still photos and video of it. They have produced plaster casts of its footprints. The self-proclaimed "Jane Goodall of the Skunk Ape," Dave Shealy of Ochopee, argues that the fact that Seminole and Miccosukee legends refer to such animals, known as mangrove or sand people, supports his belief that they walk, or more properly lurk, among us.

By far the strangest thing about this cryptid—the scientific term for the UFOs of the animal world—is the 1978 conversation about it that took place among state legislators discussing the merits of House Bill 58.

Called the Hugh Paul Nuckolls Skunk Ape Act after the District 91 (Fort Myers) lawmaker who introduced it, HB 58 set forth the following: anyone "taking, possessing, harming or molesting any anthropoid or humanoid animal which is native to Florida, popularly known as the skunk ape, or doing any act reasonably capable of harming or molesting such animal, shall be guilty of a misdemeanor of the first degree."

In response to his colleagues' ribbing, Nuckolls explained that he had been informed of numerous sightings, and people were getting concerned. After all, in the '70s, tourists were sold excursions with the specific goal of spotting and bagging their own skunk ape to bring home as a trophy.

Here is my retelling of the story of one supposed skunk ape sighting, based on a story told to Butch Wilson, director of the Clewiston Museum, by a Mr. Brown:

Mr. Brown grew up in South Bay, a city in western Palm Beach County situated on Lake Okeechobee. He and his father liked to hunt critters in his dad's gator skiff, a lightweight, flat-bottomed boat Mr. Brown Sr. had made himself. Such a skiff could easily be maneuvered with poles through the swamps.

One crystalline, star-spangled night in the early 1950s, father and son loaded the skiff on the family pickup truck as usual. They also packed their homemade gigs, or spears, fashioned with fishhooks that had been heated, straightened and then attached to the ends of flexible wooden poles.

"Ready, son?" the father asked, climbing into the cab of the truck.

"Sure thing. Where are we going this time?"

"Up north," the big man said. "To the northern edge of the Big Cypress Swamp, up in Hendry County."

"We hunting gators, Pop?"

"Nah, this time I'd like to get us some pig frogs." Pig frogs, which look a lot like bullfrogs, are found in swamps and lakes around northern Florida and other southern states.

When they reached their destination, the two hunters, one tall and one small, pulled out the skiff, spears, poles and ice chest and dragged them all over to the swamp. Then they hopped in and poled along, sweeping their frog lights back and forth in search of their prey.

"How are we going to know it's them?" the boy asked.

"Look for the twinkling eyes," his father answered. "They'll reflect the light like glowing emeralds. You'll see."

And indeed, over the next several hours, they gigged frogs right and left. The area was teeming with them.

"Gee, Pop," said the boy, dropping a frog in a croaker sack as they made their way deeper into the swamp. "This is great! Look at all them frogs!"

His father just nodded, intent on the hunt.

All was quiet until, just around midnight, a splashing sound echoed from a cypress stand. The noise grew louder until it sounded like a small army marching through the four-foot swamp water. The two stopped poling at the same moment.

"Uh, Pop?" the boy said, but his father put his fingers to his lips.

And then, to their surprise and then to their growing horror, the two hunters saw a shadowy figure emerge from the dark recesses of the trees and slowly make its way toward them. The creature's eyes reflected in the frog lights were four to five feet above the water's surface.

"Too tall to be a horse or cow," whispered Mr. Brown. "It looks more like a giant ape. But ape eyes don't glow in the dark." His son sat silently, unable to move or say a word.

Suddenly, quick as lightning, the big man turned around the skiff, and the two poled back to the point where their truck was parked. Without a word, they loaded their gear, and Mr. Brown Sr. started the engine.

"What do you suppose it was?" the boy asked when they were safely barreling down the road, their doors locked.

His father shook his head. "I don't know," he said after a long pause. "I've never seen or heard anything like it. But I'll tell you one thing, son. I've been a hunter and fisherman all my life, and day or night, I'll never set foot in Big Cypress Swamp again."

And truth be told, he never did.

## STUMPY GATORS

There have been at least four legendary Florida gators named Stumpy. The first, known as Old Stumpy, is said to have lived along the banks of the St. Johns River, at Lake George, in Putnam County. Some say he was as much as twenty feet long, the baddest gator that ever graced the shores of a Florida waterway. It wasn't all his fault. Old Stumpy got his name because somewhere along the line, he lost his left rear foot, either in a tussle with a fellow alligator or in a human trap. His permanent bad mood over the ensuing years supposedly led to his ingesting everything from dogs to mules to human beings.

Then folks in the Panama City area tell the story of another three-legged Stumpy, a beloved attraction at Saint Andrews State Park. In 2012, when no one had spotted him in Gator Lake for a while, the law went out to investigate. Turns out Stumpy had been dragged into the nearby woods, where he was shot to death and mutilated. Makes you wonder, doesn't it?

Another, more benign gator story involves a Stumpy so named for his stub of a tail. For a short time, he resided in the Terra Ceia community in the city of Palmetto, south of Tampa. Seemingly happy to mind his own business, Stumpy wanted nothing more out of life than to lounge in the golfing community's pond—and stretch his stubby legs a little on dry land from time to time.

Finally, there's the Orlando-based lawyer Gordon "Stumpy" Harris, a die-hard fan of the University of Florida Gators, who gifted the university with a statue of a giant bull gator in honor of his alma mater's football team. His nickname, he claims, came from his high school reputation as a player who was as hard to move as a tree stump.

At last report, happily, he has full use of all his limbs.

# PART II

# GHOSTS, WITCHES AND OTHER UNSETTLING STUFF

Ghost stories are so popular with audiences that many storytelling festivals—starting with the National Storytelling Festival in Jonesborough, Tennessee, considered the site of the current storytelling renaissance—give them a permanent spot on the annual program. What's more, ghost tours abound throughout the United States, with more than a few in Florida alone.

So why are ghost stories so popular? The most obvious answer explains the fan base of horror movies, as well: it's great to be scared when you know you're safe.

But I think it's more than that. I think ghost stories are, ultimately, comforting. They tell us that life continues after death. That means that untimely deaths and extreme cruelties will be avenged. And that love will last forever.

## THE GHOST OF BELLAMY BRIDGE:
### A MARIANNA LEGEND

One of the most famous of Florida ghost stories is a fascinating example of how verifiable historical events and real people become mixed up with fiction to form legend. The real Elizabeth Bellamy died of malaria in 1837, three years after her marriage and the same week as her eighteen-month-old son, Alexander. Contrary to the legend, the mansion in Marianna was not built until after her death.

The true tragic tale of the Bellamy couple was transformed by a series of coincidences. Nineteenth-century author Caroline Lee Hentz, originally from Massachusetts, wrote a novel that featured a young slave bride who burned to death at the wedding reception held for her by her mistress. The novel was supposedly based on true events that had occurred in Columbus, Georgia. Years later, in 1852, Hentz happened to move down to Marianna, where two of her children had settled. Interestingly enough, the name of the family in her book happened to be—Bellamy.

Bellamy Bridge, however, is completely real. It is one of the country's last remaining iron frame bridges of its kind. Spanning the Chipola River, it was built in 1914 on the site of the old wooden bridges dating back to 1840. Tourists take Bellamy Bridge Ghost Walks to catch sight of Elizabeth's ghost and other spectral bodies every year around Halloween.

Studying her features in the glass for the tenth time that morning, young Elizabeth Jane Croom broke into a smile. Her brother-in-law Samuel was considered the best catch in this part of North Carolina, now that his brother Edward had been snapped up by her sister Anne. A handsome medical student! An Ivy Leaguer at the University of Pennsylvania, seven years her senior! And here he was, writing to *her*!

Not that she wasn't a good marriage prospect herself, of course. After all, her father was a general. Her family was well respected in the state. But still, there were plenty of young girls from good families that Samuel Bellamy could have sent letters to.

At the thought of his latest correspondence, she shivered with excitement. "I feel so at home with you," he had written. "It is as if you and I shared the same heart. I am counting the days until I see you again."

She had read the lines so often that she knew them word for word. Now she pressed the thin pages to her chest and danced around the room. How wonderful it would be if he asked her to marry him when he came into town this afternoon! But she scarcely dared hope.

The next few hours passed in a blur for Elizabeth. After a brief time with her father in his study, Samuel steered her into a corner of the front porch. She was so excited that she nearly said "yes" before he had the chance to propose. When he did, bending down on one knee as she had pictured many times, she was so nervous that at first she stammered her reply.

"Y-y-yes!" she cried. "Oh yes, Samuel, yes, yes! Oh my darling! I will always love you! I will always love you!"

The wedding day was set for May 11, 1837. For the ceremony, Edward and Anne offered their plantation house outside Marianna, Florida, near the Georgia border, where the couple had moved not long before. Samuel was all for marrying in Marianna, where the couple planned to settle as well. But he insisted on building a mansion in town for his teenage bride-to-be. Everything, he promised her, would be perfect. Everything would be as she envisioned it. Whatever she wanted—baskets of roses, hundreds of candles, a full orchestra, a wedding gown and veil of the finest organza and lace—she would have it.

The evening of the wedding, surrounded by the cream of North Carolina and northern Florida society, the adoring pair exchanged vows. Afterward, dizzy with delight and a glass or two of imported champagne, Elizabeth danced with her new husband, her father, her brother-in-law—and then collapsed in an overstuffed chair in the front parlor. More than one wedding guest remarked on the beauty of the scene as they passed by the open doorway: the young bride, her long dark hair flung back to reveal her creamy white neck and shoulders, the hem of her luxurious gown illuminated by the glow of candles in pretty crystal holders along the floorboards.

No one knew who heard the screams first. From one moment to the next, the delighted guests were transformed into horrified onlookers. Some rushed toward the bride, others pulled back in horror as the young woman, her dress ablaze, suddenly broke through the glass doors and rolled onto the grass beyond.

Days later, Elizabeth Jane Croom Bellamy died of her burns. She was buried on the Bellamy plantation, not far from the site of the old bridge. Samuel never remarried; neither did he ever seem to fully recover from his grief. He became a banker and attended the Florida Constitutional Convention. But then, fifteen years after the death of his wife, by then an alcoholic inundated with debt, he slit his throat with a straight razor at the ferry landing in Chattahoochee.

The story of that sad love affair lives on. At first, passersby who had contact with the ghost reported her angry and vengeful. But she has apparently since mellowed. It is said that late at night, if you look closely when the moon is full, you can just make out the ghostly figure of a veiled bride floating down by Bellamy Bridge. You may see strange lights or feel a chill or strange electrical pulse. And just maybe, if you listen with your heart, you can hear the words, "I will always love you. I will always love you."

## THE BERMUDA TRIANGLE

Question: what is said to cover at least half a million square miles of ocean off the southern coast of Florida (and by some accounts as much as three times as much), yet the United States Board on Geographic Names does not recognize its existence? Answer: the Bermuda Triangle, that mysterious patch of water that links Miami, San Juan and Bermuda and has been held responsible for the disappearance of aircraft, ships and seafaring souls since as early as 1909.

Although the term "Bermuda Triangle" wasn't coined until 1964, the *Miami Herald* carried the scoop—if you can call it that—of unusual occurrences in the area back in 1950, and in 1952, a story in *Fate* magazine first identified the triangular region, which, by the way, varies depending on whom you ask. Based on Christopher Columbus's records of strange phenomena and unusual compass readings and, perhaps, a misplaced sense of proportion, believers hold up case after case of missing people (by some estimates one thousand) who ventured too near what has sometimes been called, for reasons all too clear, the Devil's Triangle.

One of the most famous cases of Triangle disappearances involved fourteen men on board five Avenger torpedo bombers in early December 1945. After taking off from Fort Lauderdale for drills, their compasses

Ships, planes and people have disappeared in the famed Bermuda Triangle. *National Ocean Service.*

suddenly went haywire, and the planes were soon lost. The mission, known as Flight 19, aka "The Lost Patrol," came to an ignominious end with the planes' losing fuel and falling, one by one, into the sea.

That was bad enough. But when rescue arrived soon after, it also disappeared. The next group of searchers looked for weeks but found nothing. The U.S. Navy's final word on the subject: it was "as if they had flown to Mars."

So what's the problem? Magnetic anomalies? Methane gas? Waterspouts? Or just an overabundance of interest in a place that is, in fact, home to no more mysteries than anywhere else?

## THE HAUNTING OF THE CLEWISTON INN

When I stayed at the Clewiston Inn, the only strange doings I experienced came from the people in the room next door partying into the wee hours of the night. But that was just my bad luck. According to a reliable local source, "many" groups of ghost hunters have verified ghostly sightings there.

The original Clewiston Inn was built in 1926 by the Southern Sugar Corporation and burned to the ground in 1937. A year later, the then-seven-year-old U.S. Sugar Company built the replacement, which stands to this day. Because sugar has long been the backbone of the state's economy, the fate of the inn's second owner is worth a closer look. Due to the Depression, Southern Sugar went into receivership in 1931, when the price of its product plummeted to a measly 1.5 cents per pound. Charles Mott, who already owned 63 percent of the company (and, incidentally, 51 percent of General Motors), purchased the rest. He renamed it the United States Sugar Corporation and went on to do rather well for himself. U.S. Sugar currently produces 700,000 tons of the white stuff each year.

"You know that old man who used to live on the second floor?" Elsie was saying to the new first-floor maid. "I was just thinking about him today. He was such a nice guy. He and his wife were so much in love."

"Sugar people?" Ruth asked, lighting her cigarette from Elsie's. She looked out over the grounds toward the bungalows behind the hotel.

"No, just retirees. They've been living here for years. He passed away awhile back, but she's still around. Anyway, you'll get to know all the regulars at the inn after a while."

The Clewiston Inn. *Boston Public Library Digital Commonwealth.*

"Is she on a trip or something? I haven't seen an old lady since I got here."

Elsie didn't answer. She suddenly realized that she hadn't seen the woman at breakfast for days. How could she not have noticed that something was wrong? This was her job, paying attention to the comings and goings of the guests on her floor.

And then she had a terrible thought. Could the woman's disappearance have something to do with the sulfurous smell she had noticed? She had been thinking the carpet was getting moldy from the last storm, but maybe—?

Without saying a word to Ruth, Elsie raced to the staircase and took the steps two at a time. She knocked on the old woman's door several times and then reached in her pocket for the master key. When the door swung open, the strong sickly odor almost knocked her down. She slammed the door shut and ran down for the manager. Together, they approached the room, holding their breaths, partly in fear, partly to fend off the smell.

What they found, in those far-off days before air conditioning, was the decomposing body of a woman who had been dead, the coroner later told them, for four days.

Over the next week, Mr. Mott quickly ordered the carpet replaced and the walls painted. Anything not painted or replaced was bleached. After a time, the room was pristine and smelled clean, if not exactly sweet.

But in the years that followed, several guests who stayed in that room telephoned or came downstairs during the night to complain to the manager, Mrs. Chris Hill, about the woman in their room. Mrs. Hill would calmly explain that a person could not have gotten in, that it was just a trick of the light. But after hours, when she was being strictly honest with herself, she had to admit that the lady in question had obviously not been ready to check out.

## THE DEVIL'S MILLHOPPER: A GAINESVILLE LEGEND

About six miles from the University of Florida in Alachua County is an ancient sinkhole, about ten thousand years old, which has been deemed a national natural landmark. At 120 feet deep and 500 feet wide, the site earned the name "millhopper" from its resemblance to a hopper, or container, that tapers downward and discharges grain onto the stone of a grinding mill.

As for the Devil's inclusion in the name, therein lie the legends. University students in Gainesville say a man once fell in and was swallowed up into the aquifer, which certainly sounds like a devilish business if ever there was one. In a tale from the nineteenth century, members of a pioneer family were taking cotton to market when they reportedly saw the millhopper swallow a stand of pine trees. My personal favorite is the story below, which features the Devil a bit more directly.

Today, the Devil's Millhopper is a popular tourist attraction, complete with steps and a boardwalk to climb closer to the stones, bones, teeth, shells and fossils below, and a nature trail around the rim—just in case the Devil still wants his due.

The Devil didn't like his view interrupted. Every day for years, he had watched a certain comely young native princess as she went about her chores. He was biding his time, he told himself, until she was mature enough to appreciate a lover of his wisdom and experience.

But lately a young man from the girl's tribe had been getting much too close to her. At first, the Devil told himself he was just a childhood playmate and the two were like tiger cubs growing up together, nothing more.

But their recent walks into the woods were a different matter. Why would playmates need to go off alone together so often? he asked himself. Where were the girlfriends she used to be so fond of? And, finally, the most worrying question of all: why were the families making wedding preparations?

The waterfall at the Devil's Millhopper, Gainesville, 1974. *State Archives of Florida/Noegel.*

The time came when the Devil had had enough. He paced his lair, trying to decide on the best strategy. Should he come up to earth in the form of a young man and attempt to woo her for himself? No, it was apparently too late for such subtlety. Should he cause the death of the young brave she fancied? No, she might mourn for him forever, and that would just make her eyes puffy and her mood less cheerful.

And, he reflected, she certainly was a cheerful girl. And so lovely. Such a nice rhythm to her step, such a gentle way about her. He had looked forward to having her at his side too long to let her go now. And so he decided, at last, to kidnap the young princess. It was, he reflected, the only way.

Not long after his decision, the Devil happened to catch the girl alone, picking flowers. No doubt for her wedding bouquet, he thought savagely. With one grasp of his mighty hooves, the Devil snatched her up and away. It was all so fast that she didn't even have a chance to scream.

Perhaps no one would have heard her if she had. But her young man, whose soul was already so closely aligned with hers, immediately felt that his lover was in danger. His heart ceased to beat for several seconds, and he felt a terrible squeezing of his chest. He gathered the other braves together, and they gave chase, even if they knew not of what prey. The Devil had a huge lead, however, and he also put to use his otherworldly powers. With a single sweep of his hoof, the earth opened under the men and swallowed them up. Still alive, they furiously fought their way back up the slick sides of the hole, but to no avail. Laughing, the Devil transformed them into the stones that lie along the walls of the crevasse.

As for the princess? She ran away from the Devil as quickly as she could and returned to the hole to look for her lover. To her horror, he had already turned to stone.

At last, the Devil saw that the princess would never love him. He could not bring himself to kill her, but he wouldn't release her, either. So there she remains, at the edge of the hole, always weeping. As soon as her tears hit the ground, the Devil turns them to stone, and they mingle with the body of her lost love.

## THE MARTIN HOUSE: A PANAMA CITY LEGEND

On a regular basis, the Rock-Tenn Paper Mill invites its employees to meetings and other company events at an old house at 119 Bayou Drive in

Panama City. The home, built in 1912 from premium-grade cypress and pine, is known as the Martin House. The company arranged to have the downstairs remodeled, but the upstairs, which is inaccessible to the public, is supposedly just as it was when the Martin family lived there, many years ago. And therein lies the following legend of horror and haunting.

"William, will you clear the dishes please?" Mrs. Martin folded her napkin and placed it alongside her plate. Her food was barely touched, but she didn't seem to notice.

Her husband, at the other end of the table, ignored the young, dark-eyed man who came to take his plate. In fact, his own dark eyes never left the face of his beautiful young wife.

She, on the other hand, looked up at the servant and smiled. Mr. Martin felt, rather than saw, the hint of a reciprocated grin on the servant's lips.

He said nothing to either of them. But late that night, he crept into the young man's room, pressed a cloth dunked in chloroform over his face and carried the limp body to the big old oak tree by the water. About dawn, when the noose was settled squarely around the young man's neck, he returned to the house.

"What? What do you want?" Mrs. Martin asked when he had shaken her awake.

"Get your shawl and wrap it tight," he answered tersely. "There's a chill in the air. Then come with me."

In silence, he led her to the oak tree. A cloud had passed over the moon, and so it wasn't until she was nearly face to face with the wretched servant that she saw what her husband had brought her to witness. By then the young man had awakened from his drugged stupor and was writhing in the noose, his feet propped on an upended log.

"But—you can't do this!" she screamed. "What are you doing? What are you thinking? Get him down this instant!"

"I think the question is what were *you* thinking," her husband replied quietly. Then he kicked aside the log, and the young man hung in the light breeze. He was dead in seconds. The woman covered her face in her hands. Then she returned to the house, weeping quietly.

Was someone watching them that night? Surely neither husband nor wife would have said a word about the incident. Yet somehow, the town whispers began, and then they grew louder, until it seemed that everywhere he went, the townspeople were staring at Mr. Martin, staring and shaking their heads and talking to their neighbors behind their raised hands and some, maybe, even complaining to the sheriff.

He knew, and yet no one dared to confront him. He had some standing in the community, and perhaps no one wanted to believe what was said. Or perhaps they were simply afraid of him. As far as he could recall, he hadn't a friend who would come right out and support him.

Finally, one day, after taking care of some business in town, Mr. Martin could stand the cold shoulders no longer. He returned home to find his wife and two young children sleeping soundly in the soft evening heat. Just as he had done once before, he pressed chloroform onto each of their faces. Then he carried them, one by one, to the big oak tree, and one by one, hanged them. And then, immediately afterward, he hanged himself.

The locals say that they have seen a black-eyed lady in white through the upstairs windows, roaming the rooms, looking for her young lover and her children. There are those who say that at one point a satanic cult inhabited the house. Others who have spent time in it report having heard thumps and screams floating down from upstairs. A young boy who broke into the house claimed he was pushed out of the window by a ghost with black eyes. Some visitors to the house simply feel menaced by ghosts; others claim to have seen a man with black eyes staring out the front window.

Is it the ghost of the wealthy Mr. Martin, or is it that of the poor servant whose life he took on the old oak tree?

## MARY'S GHOST: A SARASOTA LEGEND

Sarasota County locals have seen their share of ghosts, but none of them is as popular as the one believed to reside in the Keating Center, the oldest structure on the campus of the Ringling College of Art and Design. Built in the 1920s for the Bay Haven Hotel on North Trail, the building was purchased by famed circus owner John Ringling in 1931 and originally housed all there was of the school. Now that the college has outgrown it, the center boasts just an alumni gallery, the president's suite and other administrative offices, two floors of freshman dorms—and Mary.

Either Mary is very angry or she has a wicked sense of humor. Students report that her footsteps echo in the night, and she has been known to throw

Ghostly doings are said to take place at the Ringling College of Art and Design. *Ken Cormier, Wikimedia Commons.*

pictures from walls, lift and move objects around without their owners' knowledge, wander the halls and levitate in some of the sixty-four student rooms, particularly on the third floor.

According to the legend, Mary was a lady of the evening in the late 1920s who frequented the Bay Haven Hotel with her male clients. Maybe one of them promised to marry her and callously broke her heart. Maybe she found herself no longer attracting the right clientele due to advanced age or infirmity. Maybe she wasn't paid for her work one time too many.

In any case, Ringling's contractors supposedly found her body after the hotel was closed and they began to renovate the building. Mary had hanged herself in the third-floor stairwell, which is now a fire escape generally off-limits to students.

Unless the suicide occurred instead in room 17, as some attest. Or else room 60. On the other hand, room 46, located across the hall from the stairs, is where a young student awoke in the wee hours of the morning to the sight of a ghostly figure hovering above her bed. In another room, a young man found his hairbrush floating above his desk before it fell back down with a thud.

Mary has also been known to travel to neighboring dorms. In a Harmon Hall bathroom, a student saw ghostly female feet under a stall door. There's also the haunting of nearby Idelson Hall. According to the Sarasota History Center, a cleaning woman named Sandra spotted a long-haired spirit enter an otherwise empty bathroom she was working on—through the closed door. When the specter whispered, "Shhh" to the cleaner, the poor woman flew out of the building, never to return to work.

Would you?

## THE MICANOPY MANSION HAUNTING

If you owned a charming bed-and-breakfast establishment, would you want prospective guests to believe it's haunted? Probably not, which is why the owners of the Herlong Mansion Bed & Breakfast in Micanopy tend to play down the story a little. But it hasn't hurt business to spread the word that the building had been haunted once upon a time. That makes a stay on the premises both interesting *and* safe.

Micanopy, population just a hair over six hundred, is a picturesque town in Alachua County, situated about twelve miles south of Gainesville in the north-central part of the state. Settled in 1821, Micanopy calls itself Florida's antiques capital. The town, which is named for a Seminole chief, is rightly proud of its oak-lined Cholokka Boulevard, once an Indian trading route. The road features, along with antiques shops, its very own haunted house, circa 1845. Or so they say.

When Natalie Simonton of Micanopy married up-and-coming young entrepreneur Zeddy Clarence Herlong, there was only one thing she asked of him.

"This house," she murmured on their first night alone together. "I love this house; my daddy built it when he helped build the town. But it's got to be fixed up real nice. Promise me you'll do that for me."

"What's the matter with it?" her husband asked. "It's got two floors, and it's only fifty-five years old. Don't you like Cracker style?"

She turned to him in dismay, only to find a wide grin on his handsome features.

"Oh, Z.C.," she said, giving him a lady-like punch on his arm. "You'll be the death of me yet!"

"This house will be worthy of the queen you are," he said, taking her in his arms. "I do solemnly swear."

And so the two set about renovating Natalie's family home, not by ripping it apart, but by fashioning a fancy Greek Revival mansion around the original exterior—Corinthian columns, carriage house, pump house and all. When the work was completed to their satisfaction, Natalie and Z.C. began the happy task of bringing into the world and raising six children, four girls and two boys, who slept in well-appointed rooms with their names posted over the doorframes.

Natalie lived contentedly in that house until she died in her bed in 1950. In her will, she left the place to her six children, with the stipulation that their father would stay in it as long as he was alive.

All went well until 1960, just as the original house was turning 115. In that year, Z.C. Herlong died, and son V.J. wanted the house. But then so did daughter Mae. And Natalie (known as Pink). And also John and Dorothy and Inez. Each child wanted the gracious old mansion for him or herself and had no intention of sharing it with five siblings and their respective families. And so for nearly two decades, ownership of the house was tied up in lawsuits and countersuits. No one would agree to give up his or her claim.

And then it happened that Inez, who had married a man named Fletcher Miller, suddenly found herself a wealthy widow. As devastated as she was by the loss of her husband, she was thrilled at the prospect of ending the lawsuits in her favor and quickly made a generous offer to her siblings. At last, ownership of the house fell to her.

She was shocked at what she found. Walking from room to room after taking title, Inez shook her head in dismay.

"This place looks just terrible," Inez said to herself. "It's going to cost a fortune to get it back into the shape Mother and Father had it in. But it's worth it. All these memories!"

Inez Herlong Miller was able to make many improvements on the old house. Paint, carpentry, upholstery, wallpaper, landscaping—she spared no expense.

And then one day, by then a middle-aged mother coping with diabetes, she entered her childhood bedroom and lay down on her little bed. Some hours later, she was discovered there, comatose. Within a month, she had quietly slipped away.

Inez's son had neither the interest nor the money to maintain the house in good repair, and once more it fell to ruin. At last he sold it, and then it was sold again, and eventually it became a charming guesthouse, known both for its luxurious architecture and shaded grounds.

That's when the ghost began to make her presence felt. Various workmen around the place reported hearing the tap of light footsteps on the stairs and spoke of smelling smoke. The door in Inez's room opened and closed for no apparent reason. Guests staying in that room reportedly saw the reflection of a woman in a red shawl in the mirror. One day, a kindly looking woman appeared and then disappeared just as quickly on the verandah. Psychic researchers received strange readings in Inez's room and also at the foot of the stairs.

It is said that all these phenomena are evidence of poor Inez's ghost, eager to stay in her childhood home just a little bit longer. It's nice to think that she's checking to be sure that the place is being well cared for.

## ROBERT THE DOLL: CHILD'S PLAY IN KEY WEST

Car crashes, divorce, unemployment, bankruptcy—this is what Robert the Doll supposedly causes to those who displease him.

The story of Robert is still very much alive—even if its leading character may or may not be. It involves real, albeit deceased people in Key West, a voodoo curse and a toy forty inches tall and stuffed with wood wool, otherwise known as excelsior.

Robert has captured the imagination of Key West residents and tourists for more than forty years. And not just Key West. The doll inspired the 1988 horror movie *Child's Play* (who can forget Chucky?) and apparently receives fan mail on a daily basis. It, or he, now resides at the Fort East Martello Museum, 3501 South Roosevelt Boulevard, in Key West—just in case you care to stop by or drop him a line.

Robert Gene Otto was four years old and living with his parents in a Victorian mansion in Key West when one of the Bahamian servants told him she was going back to her country for good.

"But you're my favorite!" he cried. "I love you more than I love Mommy and Daddy!"

The young woman hugged him tightly and wept into his fine hair. She had nursed the boy when her own baby died. She had raised him as if he were her own.

"I'm sorry, child," she said. "But my people and me, we've all got to go."

"But why?" he wailed.

She frowned. "I don't know how to make you understand," she said. "We was dancing out back, and singing and praying, and your mommy and daddy didn't like it. Said we was too noisy or something."

"I like dancing and singing and praying!" the child said. "I'm gonna talk to Mommy right now! I don't want you to leave me alone!"

But when he climbed up off the woman's lap, she held his shoulders with her strong hands.

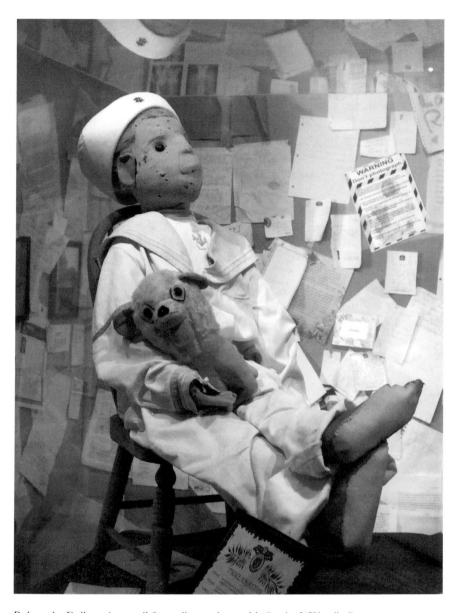

Robert the Doll receives mail from all over the world. *Cayobo, Wikimedia Commons.*

"Now you will do no such thing, little man. Haven't I taught you to behave?" Then she reached behind her back and handed him a large box. "Here. Open this. It'll make you feel better."

Temporarily appeased, he ripped off the lid and pulled out the most amazing thing he'd ever seen. It was a cloth doll, with black button eyes and a sweet little face, not unlike his own. Best of all, it was just his size. In its arms was a small stuffed lion. Or was it a dog?

"See," she said, wiping her tears with her apron. "Now, you won't be lonely without me. Your grandfather picked it out for me at a fancy store just to give to you."

The child was so entranced by the doll that he seemed to forget about the servant altogether. She watched him walk out of the room with it, totally absorbed.

At first, Robert Otto simply carried the doll wherever he went. He set it in a seat next to him at meals. He slept with it at night. He dressed it in his own sailor suit, which Mama had already said was getting too tight for him.

Before long, he began to engage in long conversations with the doll, and his mother was startled by hearing two voices when he was alone: his own and that which he supplied for the doll.

Finally, the boy announced that he was no longer to be called Robert. The doll was now Robert, and from then on he was to be known by his middle name, Gene.

Over the next couple of years, at a time when many children outgrow their dolls, young Gene Otto spent more and more time with Robert. One day, his mother came into the parlor where he had been playing with Robert the Doll and found a vase full of pansies knocked to the floor.

"Gene!" she called. "Gene Otto, you come here this instant!"

When the boy appeared, dragging Robert by his side, his mother asked, "Did you knock down this vase?"

"No, ma'am," he replied. "Robert did."

"Robert," she said, as calmly as she could, "is a doll. You are a little boy. You must learn to take responsibility for your own actions, young man."

"But it wasn't me! I swear it!"

Robert just stared straight ahead, not meeting anyone's eyes.

The doll was blamed for quite a few more mishaps over the following years, but the small town forgave Gene—who by then had become an accomplished artist and author—his eccentricities. When his parents died, he inherited the big old house at the corner of Eaton and Simonton Streets.

After his marriage, his wife, Ann, moved into the house with him. Or, to be more accurate, with *them*.

Ann Otto was glad that her new husband had made a room for the doll in the attic. She would have been gladder still had he just thrown it away, but at least she didn't have to look at it all the time. But every once in a while, when her husband had climbed up to the attic and she could hear two different voices in conversation, a shiver went up and down her spine. Still, she tried to keep her opinions to herself. Which was more than could be said for Robert.

Workmen began to hear odd noises when no one else was supposed to be in the house. Ann herself, when she had to go into the attic for the cake plate or oversized punch bowl she used once a year, would feel the doll's eyes on her. Once or twice, when its expression seemed to change from one glance to the next, she stifled a scream. At other times, people passing by on the street would report seeing a small figure move from window to window in the turreted attic room.

Had the servant woman put a voodoo curse on the doll, or was it possessed by her spirit, or both?

Gene and Ann Otto died within two years of each other in the mid-1970s. Their stately home was sold to a woman who turned it into a guesthouse, which she dubbed Artist's House, in Gene's memory. Tenants began to hear strange noises, like footsteps, as well as an occasional chuckle. Those who saw the doll said its head moved if they looked away for an instant.

When the owner sold the house six years later, she took Robert with her. Unsurprisingly, he refused to behave, so she turned him over to the Fort East Martello Museum, where for some time he lay under a sheet in a storeroom. When a photographer came to do a story on the doll for the local paper on a slow news day, he found that his camera malfunctioned.

And so the story grew. Robert was put on display, and tourists would ask to have their own pictures taken with him. Sometimes the cameras worked, often not. But on one thing everyone agreed: if they didn't ask Robert's permission for a photo or treat him with respect, something terrible would happen to them soon after. Thus began a flurry of mail, begging the doll's forgiveness and asking it to lift the curse it had put on the miscreant. Often tourists left Robert offerings, such as coins or candy, or even, since it was Key West, a few marijuana cigarettes.

These days, museum curator Cori Convertito serves as Robert's personal secretary and caretaker, ensuring that his mail is answered and his stuffing is kept in peak condition.

Does she believe the doll is possessed?

Would she speak the truth if Robert didn't want her to?

## SPOOK HILL: A LAKE WALES MYSTERY

Several explanations exist for Spook Hill, a "gravity hill" just past Spook Hill Elementary School, in Lake Wales, about fifty miles south of Orlando. Some attribute it to magnetic rock. Others say it was a spot sacred to local native tribes. Or maybe it has something to do with the city's having been built on the highest point in Central Florida. Whatever the cause, nearly everyone who has seen it has been—I believe the technical term is "freaked out."

One of the earliest stories about the site involves an African American man who parked his car at the bottom of North Wales Drive in order to catch a few bass in the neighborhood. He was on his way down to the lake when he looked back, possibly to check if he'd turned off his headlights since the sun had come up. That's when he witnessed his car rolling. Uphill.

Do cars really roll *up* Spook Hill? *Doug Kirby, RoadsideAmerica.com.*

The story made its way around the local African American community and then spread into area folklore. Eventually, it was picked up by none other than the *Wall Street Journal* and CBS News. These august news media had a different explanation: the phenomenon was in fact an optical illusion, attributable to the layout of the approach road to the hill and the surrounding landscape. In fact, cars parked on the hill don't move at all, in either direction. But they sure seem like they do.

The "fakelore" surrounding Spook Hill appears on a nearby sign: "Many years ago an Indian village on Lake Wales was plagued by raids of a huge gator. The chief, a great warrior, killed the gator in a battle that created a small lake. The chief was buried on the north side. Pioneer mail riders first discovered their horses laboring down hill, thus naming it 'Spook Hill.' When the road was paved, cars coasted up hill. Is this the gator seeking revenge, or the chief still trying to protect his land?"

The sign provides helpful instructions to experience the full effect of the gravity hill: "Stop on white line, take your car out of gear, let it roll back."

By the way, in case you didn't guess, the nearby school was named after the attraction and not the other way around.

## THE TALLAHASSEE WITCH: IT'S ALL ON THE GRAVE

This is a story based on what is known as "material culture," a term used chiefly by archaeologists, anthropologists and folklorists to refer to the objects and spaces with which groups and individuals define and represent their culture, as opposed to intangibles like songs or stories.

Evidence of the life of Elizabeth Budd Graham, popularly known as the Tallahassee Witch, is scanty, to say the least. It is based solely on an elaborate tombstone that has sat for nearly two hundred years between Park Avenue and Call Street in the Old City Cemetery, the oldest public graveyard in Tallahassee. And yet the legend lingers, certainly saying more, perhaps, about the fascination with tragic romance and mystery than about poor Bessie. It also can't hurt that the cemetery is just blocks from Florida State University's sorority row.

I've tried to incorporate all the facts and speculation swirling around poor Bessie Graham in this tale.

"She was a witch, you know." The heavyset old woman standing nearest the grave fanned herself furiously in the unseasonable heat. "There is no other explanation."

Her companion, tall and attractive, didn't turn her head to acknowledge the remark. She simply stared at the dates on the gravestone—born October 19, 1866, married November 24, 1887, died November 18, 1889—and murmured, "So young. So terribly young. And just days before her second wedding anniversary. I wonder, did it happen in childbirth?"

"Not likely, given that she had two little ones in less than two years. Although anything is possible, if you catch my meaning."

"I most certainly do not," the younger woman said. "I just wish I'd gotten to know her better."

The old woman laughed. "Then you, missie, are a fool. You already know Bessie cast a spell on your own cousin to get him to marry her...."

The second woman sighed.

"I know nothing of the kind. She was a sweet thing. Poor as a church mouse, but a dear, lovely girl. She didn't need to use any kind of witchcraft to trap our John."

"And yet you say you did not know her. From what I hear she was a poor girl, and she wanted to marry a rich man. Business was much better when they were courtin' than it has been recently."

The younger woman frowned. "Did not know her *well*. I did not know her well."

"Well *I* was the housekeeper," the old woman said, "and I reckon I knew her better than anybody. She only cast nice spells, though, I'll give her that. But I seen her workin' her magic on Mr. John, cross my heart. I was there."

"I don't believe you."

"Then tell me this," the older woman continued, taking a step closer. "Why is hers the only grave in the cemetery facing west? Completely un-Christian, if you ask me. And there's that fiddle-faddle on the stone."

The tall woman leaned over and read aloud:

> *Ah! Broken is the golden bowl*
> *The spirit flown forever!*
> *Let the bell toll! A saintly soul*
> *Floats on the Stygian River;*
> *Come let the burial rite be read*
> *The funeral song be sung;*
> *An anthem for the queenliest dead*

*That ever died so young.*
*A dirge for her the doubly dead*
*In that she died so young.*

"Why, that's beautiful!"

"Mr. John says it's by that Baltimore devil writer, Edgar Poe. Seems he wrote it about his own wife."

"And what's so bad about that?"

The woman sniffed. "'Doubly dead'? Proof positive she was a witch. Everyone knows you have to kill witches twice. And why would she float on that river instead of being taken down to the underworld?"

"You are a fantasist." The younger woman turned to leave. "But thank you for your insights."

"You're not comin' back to the house to see Mr. John then?"

She shook her head. "I think I'll walk around the graves for a little while."

"You won't find anything near as beautiful. Look at them stone vases! And the wall, and the tower! How the devil did he pay for those carved flowers and ivy? Or the cross inside the crown? Why, he owes money all over town!"

"He loved her." She leaned down once more to read, "'A dutiful daughter, a loving mother, a devoted and faithful wife.'"

"Maybe so," the older woman said, "but she was a witch through and through. I'll see you back at the house then."

The housekeeper had taken only a few steps toward the exit when, behind her, the younger woman sliced her hand through the air. At that very moment, the housekeeper tripped and nearly fell to the ground. The younger one smiled, turned back to the grave and winked.

## CARL (VON COSEL) TANZLER: FROM KEY WEST TO ZEPHYRHILLS WITH LOVE

Perhaps the strangest footnote to the story of Carl "Count von Cosel" Tanzler is the 1977 funeral notice of his long-suffering wife, Doris Anna Shafer Tanzler. Mrs. Tanzler died at the ripe old age of eighty-eight in Zephyrhills in Pasco County, her home for half a century. A former church member survived by a daughter, three grandchildren and three great-grandchildren, Doris rests in Oakside Cemetery, unlike the object of her late husband's obsession, for whom there was little repose after death.

In other words, what's so strange is just how ordinary it all is.

Although I regularly perform Mr. Tanzler's story, I was at first resistant to include it in this collection. Most of the historical facts are relatively well documented, which means it's not, according to the strict folkloric definition, precisely a legend. And I hate to think of this madman as legendary. But whenever I called on local historians to ask for story suggestions, they invariably mentioned Tanzler. It's apparently still a big story around Florida. And after all, it's not as though he killed anybody, like some of the subjects of legends included in these pages. All he did was a little grave robbing and consorting with a corpse. It's not like he intentionally hurt anyone. Right? I mean, right?


Carl Tanzler was a romantic. Doris Shafer knew that from the moment she met him in their native Dresden, Germany, when he was still calling himself George Karl Tanzler, all those years ago. She was intrigued by the man, who was twelve years her senior, with his talk of South Seas travel and his strange childhood stories about a distant relative, a countess, who had told him that she foresaw his true love, a beauty with flowing black hair. (She liked to think that she was that beauty, in disguise.) He had a dark side, too, she knew. He described to her a little of the horror of Australia's Trial Bay Gaol, where he had been relocated as an enemy alien during the War to End All Wars. Above all, however, she knew him to be a kind and thoughtful and brilliant man, a scientist and adventurer who loved and appreciated women. She had never known anyone quite like him, and she gladly married him around 1920.

In 1926, Tanzler set off for the west coast of Florida, where his sister lived, in search of better opportunities. Soon he sent for her and their two girls. But his was a restless spirit, and not long after arriving in Florida, he set off again, this time for the extreme southern tip of the state: Key West. She didn't know he was introducing himself as Count Carl von Cosel. She had no idea where he had learned to operate the new X-ray equipment or how he'd talked his way into the job at the Marine Hospital, although she suspected that his natural charm and intelligence had something to do with the latter.

Then, when their little one, Crystal, died of diphtheria in 1934, she couldn't blame him if he became a little unhinged. He was a sensitive soul, and she loved that about him, didn't she?

Although on second thought, he had become unhinged about that young girl years before Crystal's death. Maria Elena Milagro de Hoyos, known as Elena, was a beautiful, married teenager of Cuban descent. Carl's obsession bothered Doris, a lot. But how can you be jealous of a girl dying of tuberculosis? Doris had little doubt that, despite her husband's charms, the child and her parents would have grasped at anything, or anyone, to make her well. The jewels and other gifts, the constant house calls and X-ray treatments right up to her death—she understood that he did all this because he saw in her the vision of love he had had since he was a child. She didn't like it, but she understood.

She didn't know the truth until much later, of course. It came out in 1940, when the poor dead girl's sister and her family were following up some strange rumors. They told Doris about the fancy mausoleum that Carl had paid for, out of his small income. They described the late-night visits to the cemetery, every night, apparently, and the promises he had been heard to make to the grave. She withstood it all, until they told her that he brought with him to the cemetery one night a little red wagon— just like the one their girls had!—to carry the corpse back to his Key West home. She needed it repeated, again and again, even though it hurt her more each time she heard it.

By then, Carl had returned to Zephyrills and was living on his own. She really didn't mind; they still saw each other, and besides, she was used to being alone.

Then Elena's sister appeared in town to demand the corpse back, and when Carl finally gave it up, the family was stunned. He had replaced the skin with silk soaked in wax and plaster of Paris and covered it with preservatives. He had filled the abdomen with rags, fashioned a wig over her scalp and hid the odor with perfume and disinfectant. He had even put fake eyes into the empty sockets and held the bones together with clothes hangers.

Her appalled relatives took the body to a funeral home back in Key West. But Elena still had no peace. Her corpse was put on public display and visited by thousands of gaping tourists. So the family moved it as soon as they could to an unmarked grave in the Key West cemetery.

Meanwhile, Carl was found mentally competent to stand trial, but he never did. Apparently, the statute of limitations on grave robbing had run out.

There is no statute of limitations on love, however. Some have speculated that all Carl gave up was a doll and kept Elena's remains for himself. Some say her body was found on the floor of his house not far from his own.

Through it all, Doris supported her husband. He passed away in 1952, but apparently her own love didn't die until she did, a quarter of a century later.

Maybe, of the two, it was actually Doris who was the true romantic.

## THE TALE OF CHIEF TOMOKIE: BEHIND THE ORMOND BEACH LIGHTS

The forty-foot-high statue of a brave native chief stands proudly in Ormond Beach's Tomoka State Park. His name is Tomokie, and he endures for all eternity—or until the statue comes down—in the midst of being attacked by a woman with a bow and arrow, surrounded by warriors poised to avenge him. The plaque at the base of the statue reads: "Chief Tomokie: Slain by Oleeta in defense of the golden cup." The sculpture, created by local artist Fred Dana Marsh in the mid-1950s, is the concrete manifestation of a tale about a tribe that was misnamed, a man who never existed and an event that most likely never happened.

Nevertheless, scores of people have reported seeing the otherworldly lights and/or pink cloud that are sometimes associated with the story. It is said that if you drive north on Beach Street toward the park on a dark night, you may be lucky enough to see what others claim to have encountered: the Tomoka, or Ormond, Lights, often described as floating balls of light, smaller than car headlights, that suddenly appear and just as quickly vanish. They may follow motorists, or they may appear to approach a car and then separate, leaving drivers stymied as to which way to turn. They are often said to be accompanied by a low, humming sound.

Whether it is the fault of evil spirits, UFOs or just the inattention of curious motorists, the area seems to be a magnet for car crashes. The stretch of road has also spawned local legends of forbidden lovers, disappearing honeymooners and cyclists and other unsuspecting victims. And then there's something about cannibalism....

This last bit connects the stories to the odd, low-hanging pink or orange-ish cloud that is said to reside in the woods along the Tomoka River, west of Daytona. The strange phenomenon is also blamed for numerous disappearances. Swamp gas? More UFOs? Or maybe just the revenge of one very angry ghost.

In any case, "Tomoka" is most likely an approximation of the name "Timucua," a tribe that did in fact populate the land long before the European conquest.

The great chief's name was Tomokie, and he was the proud leader of the Tomoka tribe, which made its home in the rich hunting and fishing grounds between the slender Tomoka and mighty Halifax Rivers. Some said that he was too proud. The elders would complain that ever since he was a child, Tomokie could not bear the word "no." He would scream and cry and generally make life miserable for anyone who stood in his way.

When Tomokie became chief, there was no longer anyone who *could* stand in his way. And so it was that Tomokie began to do whatever he wanted. He would say whatever he wanted, no matter how hurtful. He would go wherever he wanted, even if he invaded people's privacy. He would even make strange decrees that no one understood, just because he was in charge. The members of his tribe didn't like his behavior, or him, for that matter. But Tomokie was their chief, so what could they say?

There was a sacred spring on Tomokie's land, believed to have mystical powers. For as long as anyone knew, a beautiful golden cup had sat beside that spring. No one went near the thing, however, because it was believed that only the Great Spirit was permitted to drink from it.

One day, Tomokie and his men happened to come upon the spring, hot and thirsty from a long day of hunting. When the chief stopped in front of the cup, one of the men recalled the ancients' admonition.

"I am all-powerful," Tomokie retorted. "I can do anything I like! There is no one, living or dead, who can tell me that I can't drink from this spring."

"Please, chief," they said. "Do not risk it. You will anger the Great Spirit. He will take out his wrath on all of us."

"Nonsense," he said. "The Great Spirit knows how important I am." And with that, he reached down, picked up the cup, filled it with the fast-flowing water and drank deeply.

"Delicious," he said, smacking his lips. "I am only sorry you men cannot try it. But then you are not chief."

Tomokie and his men were so intent on what was happening that they didn't realize that a maiden, Oleeta, had been quietly sitting nearby. She liked to hunt like her brothers, and her bow and arrow were sitting on the ground at her feet.

When Oleeta saw what the chief had done in the sacred waters, she didn't stop to think. She drew an arrow into her bow and, in an instant, let it fly. It landed with a small thud, squarely in his heart.

The furious braves turned on her immediately and shot her down. Then they carried both bodies back to the tribe.

Sad to say, it wasn't much later that the Tomoka people were decimated by the Spanish invaders. Was it because of Tomokie's arrogance that the tribe was destroyed?

# PART III

# LEGENDS AND LEGENDARY FOLKS

Many of the stories in this section deal with people who are part of the historical record. Nevertheless, there are always questions about people's motivations, as in the tale about Mary McLeod Bethune. And history isn't always clear on exactly what happened in a specific situation, such as who betrayed the gangster John Ashley.

What's more, there is a difference between the words "legend" and "legendary" that goes far beyond their varying parts of speech. While a legend is a story based on a factual event, person or place, we've all heard of someone or something that is "the stuff of legend"—that is, larger than life.

Remember the old Blackgama mink advertising campaign "What becomes a legend most?" Those ads were not referring to the Wakulla Pocahontas and her ilk. They meant their coats—as well as the kind of person we are proud to call human.

One or two of them are here, too.

## THE DEATH OF JOHN ASHLEY: CONFESSIONS OF LAURA UPTHEGROVE

From 1915 to 1924, John Ashley and his gang terrorized Southeast Florida banks, businesses, government entities and individuals, while becoming folk heroes to the poor Crackers who cheered on their exploits. Their crimes—

including murder, rumrunning, piracy, bank robbing and jailbreaking—led to a personal vendetta on the part of first Palm Beach County sheriff George Baker and then his son, who wore the badge after his retirement.

Even arrogant scofflaws fall in love, however, and Ashley spent the last few years of his life with an unusual young helpmeet named Laura Upthegrove. This imagined first-person account of the end of John Ashley and Laura Upthegrove gives an insight into history that maybe only storytelling can. To this day, nobody knows who gave up the Ashley Gang. Here is one version of the legend.

I loved John Ashley, and I ain't ashamed to say so. I loved him even before I ever did set eyes on him, just the idea of him. And it only got better, lovin' John. How many girls can rightly claim they were known far and wide as the queen of anything? For four glorious years, we were the King and Queen of the Everglades, and because of that, nothing that came before or after can ever matter.

Lord knows I knew what I was getting into. His pa had once been a trapper in Fort Myers who came east to Gomez—about two miles north of Hobe Sound in Martin County, down a dirt road from the old Dixie Highway—to work on Flagler's East Coast Railroad. Because the nine Ashley children grew up in and around the Everglades, John and his brothers got so they could pass through that swampland blindfolded. That made it a swell hideout, specially when ol' Sheriff Baker was hot on their trail. Maybe that's one reason they got into the business of crime in the first place. They were good ol' boys at heart, excepting maybe for their brother Bob, who even they had to admit was a mean'un.

I was twenty-four years old in 1920, with a husband and four tiny kids, one living with my ex. Nobody held me at gunpoint to get that way, mind you. I ran away with Calvin at age fourteen; he was nearly twice that. But he got me some excitement; he got me away from the same old same old that makes me want to scream bloody murder. Lord save me from boredom, I always say.

One day, I'm setting on the front porch at our home place in Pahokee, rocking baby Sidney, while my second husband was out doing whatever marine engineers do to fill their days and their pockets. The other kids were playin' out yonder. I don't know what put me in mind of John Ashley. I only knew him from the radio and the papers and from hearin' some talk now and then from my half brother Joe, who ran with him sometimes. But he

Wanted: the Ashley Gang. *State Archives of Florida.*

didn't know me from Adam. I didn't have the details, just that they'd been raisin' hell around those parts for a decade or more, what with the bank jobs, the killings, the rumrunnin' and such.

And I got to thinking: you never heard about a woman taking care of those boys, other than Ma Ashley. Who's lookin' after them? That John was a fine specimen of a man, even with the eye patch. More important, how much *life* are they living out there, on the edge of the law? And how much life am I getting, little ol' Laura Beatrice? A hausfrau!

Well, one thought led to another, and it got so bad, sitting there rockin' that baby, that I was finding it a chore just to breathe. Before I knew what I was doing, I was handin' little Sid over to my ma, packin' up a few things and taking off to find me a bank robber. Just like that. That was my way. I found somethin' I wanted and I made it my business to take it. Maybe it's because I'm such a big girl. I just ain't afraid of nothin'.

I caught up with the gang at their little island hideout near Hobe Sound called Peck's Lake in Martin County. They must've wanted to be found, because it was easy for me, although the law hadn't had much luck. And when they had, the fellas just gave 'em the slip.

John was the leader by then, of course, and I knew the minute I showed up and introduced myself that I'd have to pass muster with him. I expect I was figurin' he'd ask me to turn around, to show myself off. As I said, I'm a big girl, not much to look at, but I'm told I've got a certain somethin', a spark to my coal black eyes, a wholesome Florida tan, a way I pull back my dark hair off my shoulders—I don't know. I wasn't worried. He wouldn't need a princess, this man. He'd want someone he could count on in a pinch.

He must've been thinkin' the same thing. "Can you shoot? Can you drive?" he asked. Just that, no howdy, or nothin'.

"Sure," I said. I had brought along my old .38, and I showed him how I wore it on my hip.

John leaned back on the plain wooden bench, cupped his hands behind his head and smiled. "Guess we could try you out for a while. If Joe says it's all right."

I took to that life, as they say, like a horse to water. It wasn't long before I was driving the Ford—headlights off, mind you—through the Glades, warning them about trouble. I also picked them up from jobs and shot off like a flash, foot to the floor. But my greatest use to John, I think, was in plannin' some of our most daring bank raids. "Our." I like the sound of that. He must've, too. We fell in step one with the other like man and wife.

But for all his success, the hauls of thousands of dollars, the escapes, the love of the local moonshiners who, thanks to his pirate hijinks, didn't have to worry about the threat of foreign booze, John wasn't real sure of himself when it came to me. I never would've believed it.

It was 1924, and Joe was in jail up in Sebastian. I was worried about him. Sure, we weren't close, but we were kin. Looking back, I shouldn't have visited him so often. John put up a fuss when I got a little friendly with any of the gang. He said he didn't like my "ways" with other men. As if I would dare double-cross him! As if they would! Joe was a good-looking fella, and he had a way with the ladies, all right. Sure, we kidded around. But neither one of us was desperate enough, or crazy enough, to push it further. Especially since it was my sister Lola he was interested in.

One night I got back early from Sebastian, and I heard the boys plottin' to get on up to the jailhouse, break Joe loose and then shoot him. And God help me, that night I didn't get a wink of sleep. I just crisscrossed that campsite, left to right, right to left, trying to figure it all out. How had I gotten mixed up in this, I wondered? And why would I ever want it to end?

On the first of November 1924, acting on an anonymous tip, Sheriff Baker, who carried the grudge against John from his father who had been sheriff before him, set up a chain held by two lanterns across the wooden Sebastian Bridge, which was the only way to head north up the coast. When the Ford carryin' my precious John and three others pulled up, seven lawmen jumped out of the brush to handcuff them.

They said one of them tried to run, so they shot them all, mowed them down like so many gators. And just like a hunter, the sheriff planned to keep John's glass eye as a trophy. I managed to change his mind with a few well-placed words in the press.

When it was all over, I stayed with my mother and my babies in Okeechobee County. We were workin' in a little gas station she owned, and the boredom was killin' me. I figured I'd hurry it along and drank some iodine, but Lola got the doc to pump it out of me in time.

Then, not long after that, a couple of no-good, two-bit guys not fit to wipe John's boots gave me a hard time about some change I hadn't given them. I didn't know whether I wanted to draw my gun or just take a swig of somethin' strong.

Some say I was reaching for the rum and grabbed the disinfectant by mistake. But I knew exactly what I was doing. This was no life for the Queen of the Everglades. There was no life anywhere for the Queen, after what she'd gone and done to her King.

## "Acrefoot" Johnson: The Fort Ogden–Fort Meade Barefoot Mailman

Starting in 1845, the U.S. Postal Service designated certain "star routes," so named because they went to the lowest bidder who could provide "celerity, certainty and security," designated by three "stars" on the route register. With the creation of these routes, mail could be delivered in areas without a railroad—or even a road. While the term "barefoot mailman" for these intrepid carriers wasn't coined until much later, the men were not only authorized to travel barefoot on sandy beaches but were allowed other lapses in uniform as well, such as a canvas rather than leather mail bag.

On the east coast of Florida, folks tend to think of the barefoot mailman as the carrier on the Hypoluxo-Miami route (136 miles round-trip, once a week: 80 by foot, 56 by flat-bottomed boat). The route was handled by a succession of men between 1885 and 1892, but by far the most famous of these, James "Ed" Hamilton, disappeared in his first year of service, most likely because someone nabbed his skiff on the north side of the Hillsboro Inlet. He either drowned or was killed by an alligator.

These legendary mail carriers occupied such a beloved spot in Florida lore that Hamilton got a statue, novelist Theodore Pratt wrote a novel called *The Barefoot Mailman* in 1943 and a feature film of the book was released in 1951. The most colorful of the real-life barefoot mailmen was certainly Acrefoot Johnson, whose astonishing size, speed and energy were only matched by the man's pride and humor. And did I mention his size?

A barefoot mailman: James "Acrefoot" Johnson. *State Archives of Florida.*

In southwest Florida, there lived a man named James Mitchell Johnson who stood over six feet, seven inches in his stocking feet. He wore a size twelve shoe, so they took to calling him "Acrefoot." Weighing in at over 250 pounds, you might say he was a big ol' boy.

Acrefoot was twenty-six years old in 1877 and living with his new bride,

Margaret, near Fort Ogden when he heard tell that the U.S. Postal Service was looking for someone to carry the mail on a new route from Fort Meade to Fort Ogden, a total of about seventy-five miles each way.

He went right home to Margaret and said, "Lord knows I'm a good walker. I'm gonna go apply for that job. And I'm gonna get it, too." He leaned down to kiss her on the cheek and set off on foot for Fort Meade, just like that. By the time he arrived, there was a crowd of eager young men waiting at the post office.

You can imagine he was an impressive sight. And the post office liked that he was a married man, which made him steady.

"You know there are still some Indians on this land," they told him.

"Yessir."

"You know there's gators and snakes and all kinds of other critters, don't you?"

"Yessir."

"You know it gets mighty hot and buggy out there, don't you?"

"Yessir."

"You know we're looking for a responsible man who can protect the mail and deliver it on time, don't you?"

This time he just shrugged and said, "Yup."

Well, the competition came down to two men, Acrefoot and Big Ed Donaldson, who impressed the bosses with his reputation as an Indian fighter.

"Let me have the job," Big Ed said, "and I'll deliver the mail once a week."

The post office officials looked at one another, impressed. They were just taking out the contract for Big Ed to sign when Acrefoot leaned over and said, "I can do it twice a week. Maybe even three times, if the weather's good."

Well, there was only one thing for it. The two men would have to race from Fort Meade back to Fort Ogden, with the mail in tow. For the first ten miles, it was anyone's race. But then the big man pulled ahead. From Fort Meade to Bereah, then on to Crewsville, Dark Cow Pens, Gum Heads, Long Point, Joshua Creek and finally home to Fort Ogden.

After Acrefoot dropped the mail at the Fort Ogden Post Office, there was such a celebration that he joined in, even picking up the fiddle for a song or two when he got tired of dancing. Then he picked up the Fort Ogden mail and proceeded back on the road, where, after a few hours, he met Big Ed.

"Ah ha!" his rival said. "So you're not so fast after all, are you? I reckon I caught up."

"Reckon not," Acrefoot said. "I'm on my way back.

There are numerous stories about Acrefoot Johnson's subsequent mail career, including several in which he outwalks a horse. But beyond his speed, he was also known for his bravery.

Acrefoot kept a skiff hidden in the brush nearby any waterways he had to cross. The waters were considered too dangerous to cross without one. But occasionally, some stranger used the boat and left it on the other side.

That was the case one day when he was just leaving Fort Ogden. He stood at the river's edge, trying to decide what to do, when he saw a man waving desperately at a sailboat that had left the shore minutes before. When the man saw Acrefoot, he ran toward him.

"I can't swim," he said. "But I've got to get to that boat. If you'll swim out there and get the captain to come back, I'll give you five dollars in gold."

When Acrefoot didn't say a word, the man took out his handkerchief and wiped his brow. "I'll give you ten dollars! Just go now, please!"

Ten dollars was more than Acrefoot would see in quite a while. Without a moment's hesitation, he dove in and made his way toward the retreating boat. That's when he heard—and then turned around and saw—the three bull gators slide in and make their way toward him. It may have occurred to him that for once, something was moving faster than he was.

Then he saw the biggest of the three come toward him to get a closer look. Acrefoot didn't panic. He drew out the knife he always carried, and as the gator opened its mouth for a bite, he grabbed its upper jaw and forced it back until it snapped off in his hands. Then he stabbed the thing in the neck for good measure.

There were still two more to go. He swam as fast as he could to the boat, pulled himself up and gave the captain the message to return to the harbor.

When the schooner reached the dock, the man handed him the agreed-upon fee, saying, "What some men will do for ten dollars!" he said.

"Ain't nothing," Acrefoot replied. "I'd have done it for five."

## THE LAST DAYS OF MA BARKER: AN OCKLAWAHA LEGEND

What would Ma Barker have made of the sight of her last home floating on a barge two miles across Lake Weir in Marion County? The house, originally located at 13250 East Highway C-25, still bears the bullet holes from the infamous 1935 shootout between FBI agents and Ma and her son Freddie. But since October 2016, it has had a new resting place in the Carney Island Recreation and Conservation Area.

Legend has it that the Barker matriarch was a criminal mastermind, a story circulated by FBI director J. Edgar Hoover, it has been speculated, to justify her killing. Or was she simply a loving mother doing the best she could to protect her children, as those who knew her well insisted? Did she participate in the final shootout, still the longest in FBI history? We may never know. But we may yet learn her reaction to the sale of the property beneath the house and the structure's subsequent relocation. That's because before the move, her ghost was spotted on the front porch. But that's another story for another day....

By the time the infamous Barker gang split in 1934, Ma, who was born Arizona "Arrie" Clark in Missouri, was in her early sixties and ready to relax. In the past quarter century or so, her sons Herman, Lloyd, Arthur and Fred, along with fellow gang member Alvin Karpis and others, had killed maybe a dozen people and stolen about $2 million throughout the Midwest. Now they were mixed up in some kidnappings of prominent businessmen. Even she had had enough.

She didn't mind that the director of the FBI had called her family "the worst criminals in the entire country" or that she was the only woman to head up the Bureau's Most Wanted list (at her death there was a $100 reward on her head). All she cared about was protecting her youngest, Freddie. He was still in his early thirties, after all, and now the family had more than enough money saved up to go straight.

She left the Midwest with him and struck out for Miami, where they posed as a respectable mother and son. But they soon felt vulnerable and exposed in the big city. One day, Ma was attending a local gathering when she fell into conversation with a Central Florida woman who was visiting the area.

"Are you enjoying Miami?" the stranger asked.

"Oh yes," said Arizona, who was traveling under the name Kate Blackburn. "But I'd rather be somewhere quiet for the winter months."

"I have an idea," said the woman. "A friend of mine sometimes rents out a little place on a lake maybe four hours north of here, near Ocala. I think he's looking for a tenant."

"It sounds wonderful," Ma said. "Is it very private?"

"I'll say. It's back from the road a ways, and there's a dock out back."

Ma's eyes lit up. "My son and I would love that."

They moved in in November with a few of Freddie's friends, and the house was even better than they had hoped for. A two-thousand-square foot, two-story, wood-framed house on ten acres, it was fully furnished and even had a boat tethered to the dock. Ma was so happy she paid cash in advance for the entire winter.

"Dear Arthur," she wrote to her son back in Chicago. "Come down as soon as you can. We even have a famous gator here named Joe." Then she drew a map, indicating the lake and the town.

When the authorities picked up Arthur in Chicago two months later, they came upon the letter among his belongings. Either he was overly sentimental about his mother's correspondence or he was simply not very bright. Either way, he had unwittingly handed the FBI a very lucky lead.

It was not quite dawn on January 16, 1935, when FBI agents circled the house in Ocklawaha. They tossed three canisters of tear gas through a downstairs window.

"This is the FBI!" they cried out. "Give yourselves up! You are surrounded!"

Over the next five or so hours, an estimated two thousand bullets were exchanged between the Barkers and federal agents. When the shooting was finally over, Freddie lay dead atop a Colt pistol in the upper left bedroom with ten bullet holes in his left shoulder and chest and three bullets in his head. Ma was found nearby, felled by a single shot. The feds reported that she was curled on the floor, cradling a Tommy gun. Even in death, it appeared, she was trying to protect her boy.

Ma's familial feeling did not seem to extend to the rest of her kin, however. Her relatives didn't bother to retrieve the two bodies for another nine months.

## MARY MCLEOD BETHUNE'S INSPIRATION: A DAYTONA LEGEND

Did the extraordinary Daytona-based educator Mary McLeod Bethune have fifteen siblings or sixteen? Was her life really influenced by what a misguided child in her native South Carolina told her when she was small? And how much does it matter?

A lot is known for certain about the life of the extraordinary education activist, humanitarian and philanthropist, who lived from 1875 to 1955. The following childhood legend, whether true or apocryphal, perfectly exemplifies the power of narrative. Like the story of George Washington and the cherry tree, it reminds us what is truly important about life: not a number or a name, necessarily, but an attitude and a state of being.

"Are you coming with me or not?" Patsy McLeod stood with her hands on her hips, as little Mary Jane struggled with her shoes. She regarded her daughter with a look that was part frustration, part amusement.

"Do you want me to help you, child?"

"I've got it, Mama, I've almost got it!"

The girl always looked forward to helping her mother pick up and return the white folks' washing. Sometimes, when Mama was in a hurry or her back was feeling poorly and she didn't want to be bothered, she told Mary Jane to stay home with one of her older sisters and brothers. But today, she had said she'd be glad for the company, as long as the child could keep up.

Small as she was, Mary Jane had often heard the stories about her parents and the plantation they were walking to. Mama and Papa weren't always free to come and go as they wished, to watch their children grow up and make their own choices. They were born slaves, and although she wasn't absolutely sure what the word meant, she knew it was a terrible thing. The family still worked the same cotton fields in Maysville; it was true. But she knew Mama had bought this house with her own money, and somehow that made all the difference.

Mary McLeod Bethune. *State Archives of Florida.*

She loved helping, she reflected, as she followed her mother to what they still called the master's house. But more than that, she loved being allowed into the nursery while Mama was downstairs talking to her former mistress. There she found porcelain dolls with real hair and long lashes, stuffed animals with bodies nearly as big as the real things they were modeled after and a toy chest brimming with toys and games. She remembered the first time she was allowed into the room; she couldn't bring herself to touch anything or even to sit on the pretty rug. She had just walked from object to object as if she were visiting a museum.

But by now, she was almost at home in the place. When she was told she could go in, she skipped right over to the table with the books. She had been thinking about her choice during the long walk and decided that she had grown too old for toys. White children, she had heard one of her older brothers mention earlier in the week, read all kinds of books in school, which meant reading must be a pretty wonderful thing. She was curious to find out what was so special about it.

It wasn't until Mary Jane had picked up the most brightly colored and biggest volume she could find and sat on the floor with it in a sunny corner that she realized there was another child in the room. She was so often alone on these excursions that she had long since stopped worrying that she was intruding on the daughter of the house.

But now, a pretty, blue-eyed child a year or two older than she, with long, slender legs and blond curls skimming her waist, was glaring at her from her perch on a rocking chair. She was holding a doll that looked a lot like her.

"Who said you could be in here?" the girl demanded loudly. "I'm going to tell my mama."

"Your mama said it was all right," Mary Jane answered quickly, as calmly as she could. Mama always said whatever you do, never raise your voice to the white folks. It makes them nervous.

"Besides, I'm only here for a minute. My mama is dropping off the wash is all."

This seemed to placate the other girl, because she shrugged and returned to rocking her doll. Mary Jane was usually fascinated by other children, particularly white ones. But today she just wanted to look at this book. She lowered her eyes to the first page and found, to her delight, a pretty picture of a swan and some squiggly letters she hadn't yet mastered.

She hadn't noticed that the white child was beside her until the book was snatched from her hands, which made her jump so suddenly that she nearly fell headlong across the shining wooden floor.

"What are you doing?" the girl demanded. "Black folks can't read!"

Lucky for Mary Jane, her mother appeared at the door at the same moment. "Miss Amber!" she cried out. "Is my Mary Jane pestering you?"

The plantation owner's daughter raised herself to her full height and, without looking at either Mary Jane or her mother, left the room.

The two McLeods didn't speak until they had followed the girl out the door, crossed the long hall, descended the spiral staircase and were well on their way home. Even then, Mary Jane knew she would do well not to open her mouth, but she couldn't help herself.

"Mama?" she whispered, even though there was no one else on the road. "Is that the difference between white folks and colored? That white folks can read and we can't?"

Patsy McLeod let out a good long sigh. "You don't know the half of it, child," she said, shaking her head. "You don't know the half of it."

It is said that this experience planted a desire in Mary McLeod to study hard, go to college, become a teacher and, early in the twentieth century, move to Florida to establish the Daytona Normal and Industrial Institute for Girls. The school went on to merge with the Cookman Institute for Men in Jacksonville to become Bethune-Cookman College—she had since married and divorced—of which she became president. Bethune also founded the National Council of Negro Women and served as President Franklin Delano Roosevelt's director of the Division of Negro Affairs of the National Youth Administration.

All, perhaps, as a result of an important, if painful, lesson learned in childhood.

## BLACK CAESAR: A PIRATE'S TALE

From 1715 to 1726, as many as five thousand pirates wrought havoc in the Florida Straits and the Gulf coast. Of these, up to 50 percent were of African descent. One such pirate was Black Caesar. Or should we say *two*. Some confusion exists as to whether the infamous Black Caesar was born into a slave family on the Caribbean island of Hispaniola or was a West African tribal leader tricked into captivity by slavers. If the historical basis of both legends is to be believed, there were two pirates of African ancestry who terrorized sailors along the southern and southwestern coasts of Florida under the name Black Caesar.

The first pirate Caesar died in 1718 after throwing in his fate with an infamous colleague. The second was born into slavery fifty years later and participated in the revolt that led to an independent Haiti. For both men, piracy in the New World seems to have offered them an equality on the high seas that they could never find on land.

The following legend is about the original Black Caesar.

In the late seventeenth century, there was a West African chief known far and wide as a strong, intelligent leader. His tribe admired and respected him for these qualities, as well as because he made them rich by cooperating with the steady supply of slave traders anxious to bring back human inventory to the Americas.

The chief was so big and physically powerful that the slavers were anxious to capture him, as well. They tried all sorts of tricks, but he was too clever. During one particularly tough negotiation over price, however, the slaver with whom he was doing business felt that the chief was trying to cheat him. So he hatched a plan involving his father's gold watch.

"Your Highness," the white man said, "come see this watch. Have you ever seen anything as shiny and heavy and expensive as this?"

The chief took the timepiece with much dignity, rolling it around in his hands and holding it up to the fire to catch the light's reflection on the precious metal.

"A beautiful thing," he said. "I would like a thing like that."

"You know," said the slaver slyly, "I've got a lot more like this on the ship. And all kinds of other precious things besides. I just can't carry them off, you understand. But if you would care to take a look before we set off?"

At this, the chief narrowed his eyes. They had tried to entice him onto a slave ship before. But the other man added quickly, "With your men, of course. Bring along your strongest men."

The big chief looked from the white face before him to the watch in his hand and back to the face. Then he closed his eyes. He contemplated so long that the strangers in the circle thought he had fallen asleep. But then he opened his eyes and said, "Show me what you have. I will take my men with me."

Twenty warriors accompanied the chief onto the ship. The slaver brought out a chest with precious stones and fine fabrics. As the tribal leader was examining the pieces, one by one, the ship began to move, slowly, slowly, away from the dock.

Suddenly, the chief jumped up. "You have left the shore!" he screamed. Then he and his men lunged toward the port side of the boat, but it was too late. Each one had the arms of a white man around his body and the barrel of a gun to his temple.

And that is how the chief was captured.

There in the hold of the ship with the other screaming, sweating human cargo, he vowed to take his revenge, whatever the cost. The opportunity came much sooner than he'd expected. En route to the Spanish Main—the land under Spanish control that bordered the Gulf of Mexico and the Caribbean—the ship was swept up in a massive hurricane, and along with a white sailor he'd befriended onboard, the chief sailed away in a longboat loaded with weapons and ammunition. The pair made their way to the eastern side of the upper Florida Keys, on a small swampy island called Elliott Key. Using the island as a base, they began a steady business posing as shipwreck survivors. Each time a friendly captain ordered them rescued, they turned around and robbed the crew.

Whether the chief took on the name Caesar, which is Latin for king, from something he heard or whether the men gave him the name is not known. But Black Caesar, as he was soon called, took to piracy as if he'd done it all his life. He and his men preyed on passing ships, often tying them to the rocks and sinking them. Eventually, they brought their spoils to one of the small islands north of Key Largo, not more than seven miles from the mainland, which became known as Caesar's Rock. Especially cruel to their male captives, they were known, despite building a prison in the area, for coining the expression "Dead men tell no tales."

It is said that he treated women quite differently, maintaining a sort of harem of one hundred females on Elliott Key until he moved it west to Sanibel and Captiva. (Note the similarity here with the tale of Gasparilla.)

This wanton plundering of ships went on for about a decade, with Caesar moving back and forth between Biscayne Bay and the Gulf, until he decided to join forces in the mid-Atlantic with the famous English pirate Edward Teach, more commonly known as Blackbeard.

In 1718, Blackbeard lost his life in a battle with the British Royal Navy at Ocracoke Island, North Carolina. Caesar had agreed to blow up the ship if they found themselves captured. But before he could prepare the gunpowder, the sailors surrounded him.

He was taken to Williamsburg, Virginia, and, after a brief trial, met his death at the end of a rope.

## THE NAMING OF BOCA RATON

Ah, luxurious Boca Raton by the sea! Among the romantic tales that swirl around the southernmost city in Palm Beach County is that of the pirate Blackbeard's kicking back in the waters of Lake Boca Raton between raids, and then, after his death, returning as a seagull—you read it right—to guard the treasure he'd hidden under a gumbo limbo tree. The Blackbeard legend got an extra boost in the 1920s, when the crew building the beach

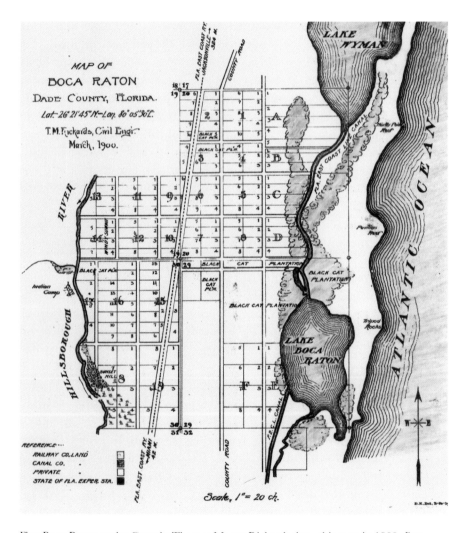

First Boca Raton settler Captain Thomas Moore Rickards drew this map in 1900. *Boca Raton Historical Society and Museum.*

road known as Highway A1A discovered a couple of gold doubloons in the sand. That find led all manner of wreckers to search the ocean floor for the remains of a ship supposedly carrying silver bars. As of this writing, however, no one has gotten filthy rich from the hunt.

The unlikely name of such a paradise has likewise captured the imagination. Does "Boca de Ratones," often translated as "rats' mouth," refer to the inlet where ships could alternately be buffeted by its crags or harbored against the winds? Or, following other interpretations of the Spanish, does it mean "hauling inlet," that is, shallow waters available only to smaller boats that could be pulled through? Or is the true translation "thieves' inlet," due to the above-mentioned spate of pirate tales connected to the area?

The answer to that last question, at least, seems to be: yes and no. Apparently there was a second Boca Raton, or rather a first, in what is now Indian Creek on Biscayne Bay, in Dade County. The pirate Blackbeard and his associate Black Caesar may indeed have plied their trade in the waters of *that* Boca Raton.

As for the present-day Boca, as the locals call it, historians tell us that its lake and inlet were usually closed to shipping, due to their as-yet-undredged sandbars. Between the 1820s and 1850s, both names were listed on maps of the area, which explains why the mix-up persists to this day.

Which leaves us with a begged question. Does the fact that present-day Boca Raton was named for the former Boca Raton mean we can't know the true source of the name?

Again, yes and no. Take your pick from the stories above. All I know for sure is that the nickname "Botox Raton" has something to do with the town's apparently ageless residents.

## THE MANY NAMES OF CAPE CANAVERAL

What's in a name? These days, the words "Cape Canaveral" elicit images of astronauts and spacecraft on launching pads. But long before the arrival of Ponce de Leon, in the vicinity of what is now the town of Melbourne Beach, the Ais and the Timucua peoples were enjoying a prosperous life off the seafood and vegetation on the nearby promontory.

The native peoples didn't take too kindly to the Spaniard's visit. In fact, the explorer was just able to pick up some much-needed provisions before

No spacecraft dot the pristine landscape in this view of Cape Canaveral Beach. *"Cape Canaveral—Atlantic Ocean Beach (2)" by Jared is licensed under CC BY 2.0.*

beating a hasty retreat. It's said he named the area "Corrientes" for the shipwreck-inducing currents, but maybe he was thinking of another kind of wreck altogether.

Nobody knows for sure why the land separated from Merritt Island by the Banana River was ultimately named Canaveral. What may be the first map containing the name "Cabo Cañaveral" dates back to 1564. *Cañaveral* in Spanish literally means "canebrake." It is said that when Francisco Gordillo came ashore in 1520, he was attacked just like his predecessor had been seven years earlier. To the Spanish, the local bamboo reeds the natives sharpened to fashion arrows used in both incidents resembled sugar cane.

In any case, the name stuck for four centuries. Then, one week after John F. Kennedy's assassination in 1963, his vice president and successor, Lyndon Baines Johnson, renamed the area Cape Kennedy. It took ten years for the Florida legislature to do what Florida residents had lobbied for all that time: they voted to change back the name, however it got there in the first place.

## Al Capone's Parties: A Miami Legend

On April 21, 1986, the TV journalist Geraldo Rivera appeared in a two-hour special broadcast called "The Mystery of Al Capone's Vaults." As many as thirty million people nationwide watched Rivera unlock a recently discovered vault in Chicago's Lexington Hotel. The vault had belonged to the notorious gangster, who had died forty-one years before. Rivera's haul: several empty bottles and a pile of dirt.

And so, the question remains: what actually did happen to Scarface's $1.3 billion fortune after he died, in 1947, of a massive stroke in the second-floor bathroom of his Palm Island home? His lifestyle was known to be decadent, but certainly there was plenty of cash to go around. Many believe he buried the money for safekeeping, perhaps on his property. The ill-gotten loot has never been found.

The following legend swirls around the high-flying lifestyle of one of the country's richest and most famous gangsters. This one involves no less than a president-elect—and leads to the mobster's downfall.

Gambling, alcohol, prostitution and murder had been very good to Al Capone. By age twenty-nine, the young mob boss was able to winter in Miami, not far from the casinos of Cuba or "Vegas South," as nearby Hallandale was known, but more than 1,300 miles from his Chicago haunts, where his reputation for mayhem had begun to cramp his style.

First, he stayed in area hotels, then he rented an apartment. But before the year was out, he paid $30,000 for a seven-bedroom, five-bathroom Spanish-style house. The address was 93 Palm Avenue, on the very private man-made Palm Island in Biscayne Bay.

Lovely as it was, what with its lily pond and grotto, palm trees and guest quarters, one of the property's main features was an enormous swimming pool and two-story cabana, hugging the bay. At thirty by sixty feet and holding sixty thousand gallons of water, it was the perfect party location, and the mobster's parties were known far and wide, as much for their guest lists as for their extravagance.

"Do you know what our weekly meat bill is?" his wife, Mae (also known by her middle name, Josephine), asked one night after a party. Mae had been a sales clerk when she met her husband and hadn't become Mrs. Capone until after the birth of her son Albert. A Brooklyn girl from an Irish family, she was a beauty, true movie star material. But despite her husband's wealth and

Arrested in Miami: Al Capone's mug shots. *Miami Police Department, Wikimedia Commons.*

connections, she would never be seen on the big screen. Mae was a private person, happy to be with friends and family and out of the limelight. She would have preferred a faithful husband—one who did not give her baby son syphilis-related deafness—to her life of luxury.

She didn't bother to wait for a reply: "$250."

"Really?" He was fixing himself a drink at the bar. "Can you beat that? I wonder what our liquor bills are?"

"It's all these parties," she continued, lowering herself into a chair by the pool. The moon was out, and its reflection on the water made her think of a giant pearl, floating just below the surface. "The neighbors are complaining."

At this, he turned to face her. "Neighbors? What neighbors are complaining?"

She frowned. "We got a formal request from the J.C. Penneys to keep the noise down."

"The Penneys! Why, they live all the way over on Belle Isle!"

"Who knows?" She inhaled deeply from her cigarette. "Sound carries."

He shrugged and sipped his drink. "I imagine the Penneys couldn't care less. Seems to me they have a famous guest staying with them, and that's the problem."

"But Al, Herbert Hoover is the president-elect! We should have more respect!"

"Hogwash. I'm richer than he is and more powerful than he is. End of story."

As it turned out, that was not the end of the story at all. Legend has it that Hoover was so annoyed by the noise of Capone's drunken revels while he was staying with the Penneys that he decided to make the mob boss's arrest a top priority of his government. If the stories are true, it was not gambling, alcohol, prostitution and murder that caused the U.S. president to demand the arrest of Capone by any means, even, finally, tax evasion. It was the noise from those fabulous pool parties.

Maybe old Scarface should have invited him.

## FLAGLER'S FOLLY: "THE EIGHTH WONDER OF THE WORLD"

Henry Flagler's statue resides in St. Augustine. *State Archives of Florida.*

The "story" in this brief history rests squarely in the word *folly*. What was crazy about the obscenely wealthy Henry Flagler's spending up to $50 million of his own money—$1 billion in today's dollars—to extend his already successful railroad line from Miami over land and water to Key West, when at the time the destination city was the largest in the state? When work commenced in 1905, Key West was an important gateway to Cuba, just 90 miles away and a recently acquired trading partner as a result of the Spanish-American War. The city was a bustling center of cigar makers and fishermen, spongers, merchants and mariners, less than 150 miles from the tip of the U.S. mainland. Moreover, it was the nation's closest port to the Panama Canal. And besides, the train would run on fuel from Flagler's own Standard Oil, rather than coal, giving him a steady, and reasonably priced, supply. It looked like a terrific investment.

What could possibly go wrong?

Insects, for one thing. And swampland. Then there was the weather. It was the Labor Day Hurricane of 1935 that finally did in the line, which had been operating at that point for twenty-three years. The Overseas Highway, or U.S. 1, was built over the old viaducts and trestles in the 1930s and got a much-needed overhaul half a century later. And in 1979, the old remnants of Flagler's Folly were added to the National Register of Historic Places.

So maybe he didn't do it for the money. Maybe Henry Flagler, age seventy-five the year work on the line commenced and dead the year after it was complete, had something else in mind for what was known at the time as the eighth wonder of the world.

Maybe it was all about his legacy, after all.

## JOSÉ GASPAR: A TAMPA PIRATE

Since 1904, the Gasparilla Festival in Tampa has proudly celebrated—and since 1911 actually staged—a fictional battle, the outcome of which didn't even occur in fiction. The play-acting opponents are a pirate fleet commanded by a Spanish naval officer gone rogue named José Gaspar and the U.S. military. Their supposedly real-life battle is said to have taken place at the same spot in Tampa Bay in 1821.

During the staged invasion, which occurs every year on the last Saturday in January, scores of volunteer pirate ships unload their crews, kidnap the mayor and hold him hostage until he hands over the key to the city. But the fun doesn't stop there. The next two days are filled with partying, parades and plenty of alcohol.

No historical documents have ever been able to confirm the existence of José Gaspar. More to the point, there was apparently very little piracy of any kind in the Tampa Bay area during his supposed reign of terror. In fact, the source of the tales appears to have been a local tall yarn spinner named John Gomez and a 1900 railroad advertisement that elaborated on his tall tales.

The one thing we know for sure? Only the most foolhardy of sailors would dare stand alone on a ship's deck in the midst of Tampa Bay. That's because locals say José Gaspar's eyeless, seaweed-encrusted, anchor-chained ghost only emerges from the sea to drag a sailor back down with him when no one is there to witness it.

There is no nice way to say this: as a child, José Gaspar was a coddled, arrogant scamp. With his good looks and manners, dark, penetrating eyes and slender build, he could usually charm his upper-class parents out of

Gasparilla Festival pirates make merry in Tampa. *State Archives of Florida.*

punishment for his misdeeds—and into raising his allowance. No one else seemed to be quite as forgiving.

The allowance was, in fact, what started it all. Near Seville, Spain, where José was born in 1756, well-to-do families gave their scions plenty of pocket money. José, however, was one of those children who always wanted more.

That's when he hit on his big plan. He invited for lunch a pretty, blond neighbor and at the end of the day refused to let her go home. The note he sent to her family read: "If you want to see your daughter alive, you will deliver to me 100 gold pieces wrapped in a black cloth." He then signed his name and address, which in hindsight probably wasn't the smartest strategy for a kidnapper.

In his defense, he was only twelve years old.

José's father and mother tried everything to calm the girl's horrified parents, but they took the matter to the local magistrate anyway. In that land and in those days, judgment was swift. The rapscallion could either enter the naval academy or rot in jail. His tearful mother hugged him on his way off to the academy.

"Try to behave, my beautiful Gasparilla," she begged. "If you do not, I fear that you will endure a life of great hardship."

José shrugged her off and waved a hearty goodbye. Then he boarded the carriage that would take him off to his future. In truth, it didn't feel like much of a punishment to him.

To everyone's surprise, the wild José excelled at school, rising quickly due to his wits and bravery from cadet to lieutenant and then eventually admiral of the Atlantic and finally, at the tender age of twenty-seven, naval attaché at the court of King Charles III.

It is said that Gaspar married well, and the couple had a child. He might have lived out the rest of his life in wealth and honor and been remembered as a respected military man. But the more powerful he was, the more interested he was in romantic entanglements outside of his marriage.

There was one woman in particular, the king's daughter-in-law, no less, who took his casual flirting more seriously than most. One warm summer night, while the two were dancing at a royal ball, she demanded that he run away with her.

He started to laugh. "Why on earth would I do something so stupid as that?" he asked, never one for diplomacy. "I have everything I want here: money, position, power, the king's ear. Why would I give that up?"

The young woman squeezed his hand tightly. "Why, so we could be together all the time, of course! Not just when you can escape your wretched wife." Here she pouted prettily. "And your other women at court."

Gaspar stopped dancing. "And die of boredom?" he scoffed. "What kind of fool do you think I am?" He left her there in the middle of the floor, humiliated among the other dancers, to make her way to her seat alone.

The callow young man forgot the encounter as soon as it occurred, but not so his paramour, who had the ear of the Crown. Within the week, the king had him arrested on trumped-up charges that he had stolen the crown jewels. Soon after, his home was burned to the ground, and his mother, wife and baby all died in the blaze.

It seems that Gaspar needed no further motivation to revolt. Swearing vengeance on the king, and thus on all of Spain, he escaped his shackles and set out to sea on a ship called the *Florida Blanca*.

After a time, the ship's captain ordered the schooner farther out to sea to protect it from the fighting between Spain and Britain. Gaspar and some of his fellow sailors, hungry for adventure, plotted and then executed a mutiny. Wresting control of the ship, they changed course and sailed for the West Indies and the Gulf coast of Florida. There, Gaspar proclaimed himself captain and set up base camp on the northernmost island in Charlotte Harbor, near present-day Fort Myers. Three other small islands dotted the mouth of the harbor as well, but the area was mostly uninhabited.

"They're going to be looking for the ship," his first officer told him over a bottle of rum on their first night in the harbor.

"I've been thinking about that," Gaspar said. "As captain of this brig, I am rechristening it the *Gaspar*. No, on second thought, let's call it *Gasparilla*. 'Little Gaspar.' That's what my mother used to call me.

"Yes," he continued, rising to his feet and starting to pace, hands behind his back. "I like that. *Gasparilla*. In fact, I am going to take on that name, too. And while we're at it, let's name this island Gasparilla. It makes me happy to think of my dear, sweet mother back in Seville."

For the next four decades, Gasparilla and his men preyed on unsuspecting ships en route from the west coast of Florida to Cuba. During his long career, he gained a reputation for a strange mixture of cruelty and gallantry. On one hand, he told his men to take the female captives to the island he named Captiva and hold them there for their own pleasure. Yet the same man sentimentally named Sanibel Island after the lost love of his first mate, Roderigo Lopez.

One of the many ships the pirates plundered held an important passenger, a very young and very beautiful princess named Useppa. From the moment he laid eyes on her, Gasparilla was smitten. He wasted no time in making advances to her, all of which she spurned. Yet the more she defied him, the more he wanted her.

"Please leave me alone, señor!" she implored him. "My heart belongs to another. I am engaged to be married!"

"No man or woman says no to Gasparilla!" he stormed. "If you defy me, I will have you beheaded at dawn!"

"Then do your worst," she said quietly. "But I will go to my death an unsullied woman."

He didn't know why she angered him so; he had had so many women and would have many more. Perhaps there was something in her arrogance that reminded him of himself. He reached for his scabbard, pulled out his knife and sliced her throat. At the sight of the dark blood streaming from her lifeless body, he fell to his knees and wept. He buried her himself on a small island in the harbor and named it after her.

It was not long afterward that Gasparilla told his crew he planned to retire. His heart was broken, and he was sixty-five years old. He'd had a longer and more successful career than any pirate of his acquaintance. He knew the time had come.

But then, just as the crew was saying their farewells and discussing the best way to divide the loot, the lookout called to them. A British merchant vessel had just appeared on the horizon.

One final act, he thought. Might as well go out in style.

They approached as they often did, planning to slip between the ship and the wind, when the British vessel manuevered around them. Then, to the pirates' horror, cannons appeared on the deck, and the ship dispersed of its British colors and raised the Stars and Stripes. This was the navy schooner known as the USS *Enterprise*, under orders to clear the area of pirates by any means possible.

Shots were fired, and Gasparilla's vessel was sinking into the Gulf before the stunned men could make a move. He was the first to shake himself out of his stupor. Running up the bow of his ship, he cried out, "Gasparilla dies by his own hand!" And the last anyone saw of the last buccaneer, he had wrapped an anchor's chain around his belly and was jumping overboard, sword raised in defiance.

Some say Gasparilla ordered his men to send twenty chests of treasure up the Peace River by longboat in order to bury them along the swamps and waterways. Others claim the loot, worth $30 million, traveled by mule train up to New York.

Only his ghost knows for sure.

## THE ORIGINS OF KEY LIME PIE

You can't get much more "Florida" than Key lime pie. With ingredients like condensed milk, eggs and good old Keys citrus (which, incidentally, is green when picked, yellow when ripe), and topped with gobs of whipped cream, the unusual sweet-and-sour dessert is a state treasure. Likely due to the pie's importance, several origin stories are in circulation. It seems that when it comes to Key lime pie, everyone wants to get in on the act.

Some trace the origin of the yellow-and-white dessert to a Key West botanist at the turn of the twentieth century by the name of Jack Simons. Others attribute the recipe to Aunt Sally, the cook who worked for nineteenth-century millionaire wrecker William Curry. Famed Key West ghost hunter David L. Sloan claims he stumbled across the recipe in the pantry of the Curry mansion and was so shocked and delighted that he forgot all about exploring the possible supernatural activity on the floor above.

Chances are that the recipe actually originated with local sponge fishermen. Due to their long stints at sea, the spongers stocked up on basics that wouldn't easily spoil and would contribute to their general health—hence the canned sweetened condensed milk, the limes (the old seafaring

Key lime pie may have kept sailors in the pink. *"Key Lime Pie at Coastal Kitchen" by Ralph Daily is licensed under CC BY 2.0.*

preventative for scurvy) and eggs. The original recipe did not require baking, and few at the time seem to have worried about salmonella, so an oven was not required.

Today, however, it is usually recommended.

# GRAYCE McCOY: A SEBRING LEGEND IN HER OWN TIME

The most interesting parts of outrageous Sebring realtor Grayce McCoy's life are absolutely, verifiably true. The part-Cherokee native of Pea Ridge, Georgia, was larger than life, and so are the many stories folks around town still tell about her. Sharp as could be with a flair for style and a heart brimming with generosity, Grayce still wasn't everybody's cup of tea. But the Lady in Pink certainly helped put Sebring on the map, and no one who knows her story can ever forget her.

Grayce McCoy loved pink, and she was wearing it the day she arrived in Sebring, in 1955, with her military man husband. At the time, no one thought one way or another of either the color or the woman.

But she took to the place right from the start. The military economy had started Sebring booming again after the Depression. The little town was blossoming, and she had arrived in its springtime.

Speaking of blossoms, not long after her arrival, Grayce, on the lookout for something to occupy her time and her active mind, decided to purchase some groves and an apartment house. She was an independent woman in an era when not many were, having already made plenty of money prior to her marriage with her own successful theater and portrait companies.

Grayce came home from buying the real estate exhausted and happy, stepped out of her pink pumps, undressed, showered and fell right to sleep. Then, sometime in the middle of the night, her eyes flew open. Was it a dream that had awakened her? A noise outside? More likely only a feeling inside. She knew at that moment just what she had to do. She would become a realtor.

The next day, Grayce got hold of a real estate manual and set about memorizing it. That's how she was. Before you could say, "Open for business," she was open for business. Her first office was little more than

Grayce McCoy outside her Sebring office. *Sebring Historical Society.*

a cubbyhole at the Sebring Hotel, but she didn't mind. She went around knocking on doors, and in her second week, she sold a $175,000 ranch to a man from nearby Lorida. Within six months, she had already resold the same property to Westinghouse. It wasn't the hard sell that made her shine, she always said. She made friends easily, and friends want to do business with friends. It was as simple as that.

Grayce's real estate business quickly prospered. And the more flush Grayce got, the more pink was in her life. She posted pink-and-black signs all over town that read, "Deal with the Real McCoy." Her first real office, downtown on the Circle, was painted pink. She purchased a house, a nice property on Lake Jackson, and she painted that pink, too. She bought several Cadillacs and a Jeep, all pink, like the real estate she started picking up downtown. People around town even started to call the color "Grayce Pink." She bought herself an ocelot for a pet. The big cat may or may not have been pink, but she did dye her poodles. Unfortunately, the stuff made their hair fall out.

To add to her pizzazz, Grayce took to wearing pink or Marilyn Monroe blond wigs. Over the years she bought hundreds of them, and she paired them with flamboyant hats, furs, boots, jewelry and rhinestone sunglasses. She also bought two mobile home parks, which she dubbed Grayces and Grayces II. Now she owned hundreds of homes on Highway 27, and she painted every one of those units pink.

She worked hard, doing whatever she had to for a sale. One day, she took several men to see some ranchland. The ride was over miles of bumpy, unpaved roads.

"How can you drive that Cadillac over these ranch roads?" one of them asked. "Aren't you worried about doing damage to the car?"

"Honey," she said. "It's these ranches that bought me this Cadillac!"

Following that work ethic, Grayce traveled anywhere there was land to sell. One day, she called her husband at work.

"I'm going to Costa Rica," she announced. "I'll be home Friday."

"Why didn't you tell me this morning?" he asked.

"I didn't know this morning, honey," she said. "The opportunity just came up."

"But you have to come home to pack."

"And arrive there later than anyone else? I'll buy a toothbrush in the airport."

What she also did in the airport was address a dozen or more envelopes to her male clients. When she arrived at her destination, she'd have someone pick up for her some dirty postcards. She would write on them just one word: "Dis-grace." Her little joke.

Some folks in the conservative town didn't like her raunchy sense of humor, but she didn't care. She once negotiated a $2.5 million deal for a client to buy the Kenilworth Hotel and Golf Club from its owner, Frank Rose. After the deal was signed, her lawyer said, "So Grayce, how does it feel to make so much money in just one day's sale?"

She laughed. "One day's sale? That's a good one. Listen, sonny, I've been kissing Mr. Rosebaby's ass for fifteen years."

From the other end of the table, Frank Rose shook his head. "Grayce," he said, "I think if you and I were in bed together, you'd still call me Mr. Rosebaby."

She had become such a celebrity by then that some folks bought from her just to say they had. Besides, she had a reputation for playing fair. In 1968, she was named Sunshine State Information Bureau Woman of the Year in real estate and development. The plaque read, in part: "This award honors over a decade of creative real estate sales and development, which have been instrumental in the growth of Central Florida and Highlands County."

The accolades were great, but what really mattered was the work. As head of a group interested in adding additional lanes to U.S. 27, Grayce marched right into the statehouse in Tallahassee at the front of the contingent. It was a battle she said she particularly enjoyed winning.

Eventually and inevitably, the IRS came to audit her and asked about the Cadillacs.

"They're not for personal use, are they?" the agents asked.

"Oh, no," she said. Acting on a tipoff, she had sent her Grayce pink cars home with her employees the night before. That morning they were returned, all seven of them in a row. Needless to say, she got through the audit just fine.

Grayce may have cheated the IRS, but she was more than generous with her money and her time. There was a place in town that housed abused and unwanted children, and she stopped by often to talk to the girls and bring them things they needed from the drugstore and elsewhere. She encouraged them to have dreams and to set about reaching them. Look at her, she told them. She had started from nothing, and now she had so much.

By the mid-'70s, Sebring was going strong, thanks in large part to Grayce McCoy. The town was expanding beyond the city limits, with development in unincorporated Highlands County.

When did it start to get too much for her? She went through a terrible divorce, for one thing, and the terms of the settlement meant that she had to sell her mobile home parks. Losing them was like losing a part of herself.

It got to the point where she could only find peace in Cherokee, North Carolina, where her people were from. She loved those majestic mountains, which no one could ever really buy and sell. Not even her.

But she always returned to Sebring. She passed away at Highlands General Hospital in the fall of 1977. No one knew her age for sure, but they guessed her to have been in her mid- to late sixties.

One editorial read, in part: "When Grayce McCoy died last week, Sebring lost its most colorful attraction. Hard-headed and warm-hearted, the Lady in Pink has left her mark on the area, and it will never be quite the same."

The piece ended with these words: "There will never be another in this world of stereotypes and button-down minds. The Pink Lady is gone, and long after the last flame of flaming pink buildings has faded under Sebring's blazing suns, there will be those who remember the woman who gave as much life to the town as the Race."

As she always said, she didn't care what they said about her, as long as they remembered her name. And remember they will, for a good long time.

## BONE MIZELL: THE CRACKER COWBOY

Ruby Leach Carson told the story of the rib-tickling Cracker cowboy in her poem "The Ballad of Bone Mizell," which appeared in *The Florida Teacher* in 1939 and was later set to music by Jim Bob and Dottie Tinsley. Quite a few cowboys have been immortalized in cowboy poetry, but few were honored with both a poem *and* a painting by a famous artist.

So what exactly is a Florida Cracker? Although sometimes it is used in a derogatory sense, the designation "Cracker" is also worn with no small amount of pride by white, rural Floridians of Scots-Irish or English descent—including two former Florida governors and a current senator—whose ancestors probably herded cattle on the land ten generations ago or more. The word is believed to have derived from the whips used by these southerners on livestock and, at times, slaves. Other theories hold that it comes from the Old English *crake*, meaning to brag, or perhaps from the ancient Scottish term for a class of people unpopular with the ruling elite. In any case, Bone Mizell certainly fit the bill.

His parents named him Morgan Bonapart Mizell, but everyone knew him as plain old "Bone." As time would tell, the nickname could equally well have stood for "funny bone" as for Bonapart. Born in 1863 in the one-horse town of Horse Creek, Bone spent the better part of his fifty-eight years on earth in and around Arcadia, about 150 miles north of Fort Myers, working as a cowboy.

He herded livestock for some of the most powerful cattle barons in DeSoto County, including Ziba King, who over the years became such a friend and supporter that he agreed to bail the long, tall drink of water (six feet, five inches in his stocking feet) out of more than a few scrapes in his checkered career. Judge King's assistance was required because not only was the lisping, unschooled Bone an expert with a whip and a terrific horseman, but he was also, by all accounts, a cattle thief, liar, gambler, booze guzzler and general scalawag.

There are at least two reasons that Bone Mizell was lauded during his life and is still remembered nearly a century after his death. For one, the great American painter Frederic Remington captured his likeness on canvas in 1895 as the quintessential *Florida Cracker*. At least as important, though, was his own art form: humor. When Bone opened his mouth, he had everyone who knew him in stitches, be they partners in crime, lawmen or victims.

Frederic Remington's painting of Bone Mizell, entitled *A Cracker Cowboy*, 1895. *Wikimedia Commons*.

Bone's bon mots were such a hit that he gave new meaning to the term "Cracker"—as in wisecracker.

One of the best-known stories about Bone Mizell concerns the death of a close friend and fellow cow hunter, John Underhill, who shuffled off this mortal coil while riding the herd near Kissimmee. Hearing of the loss, Bone took some time to do what he always did to commemorate news both good and bad: he had a few snorts. On his return from the bar, he found several of the other cowboys busily bathing the corpse.

"What do you think you're doing to ol' John?" he barked.

"Why, Bone, we're only washing the body, dressing him up for the burial. It's just customary."

"Leave him be!" Bone demanded. "John never washed hisself in life; he certainly doesn't have to put up with it in death!"

So the makeshift funeral took place, with the body, shall we say, less than savory. The cowboys buried their friend in a lonely grave out in the brush. And that would have been the end of the story, except that some little while later, a young traveler from New Orleans, sick in body and soul, crossed Bone's path. The two took a shine to each other. Some of the more cynical types said the stranger, who had a few coins in his pocket, kept Bone's whistle wet. Others said the older man felt some sort of responsibility to help heal the newcomer by introducing him to the healthy outdoors life. Whatever the reason, the younger man didn't last long, and it fell to Bone to dispose of the corpse.

It was summertime in south central Florida, and the merciless heat made it next to impossible for Bone to drag the body back to Arcadia for a proper burial. Instead, he dug his new friend a grave right alongside his old buddy John. Maybe he thought the two would keep each other company. He mumbled a few words at the grave site, perhaps to that effect.

But that's not the end of the story, either. Some years later, the young man's family got wind of his untimely demise. They sent Bone funds to ship the body back home for a proper burial in their own plot. Not one to waste perfectly good cash money, Bone used it to toast to his pal in style. Then he toasted again. And again.

When he emerged from the ensuing haze, the grizzled old cowboy still felt obligated to send a body home to the poor boy's family. And here's when he got to thinking. Side by side lay two corpses, that of his pal John and that of the young man from New Orleans. The former had often confided in him that he had a hankering to travel but, due to this and that, had never gotten the chance. The latter was so world-weary that he had claimed more than once that he didn't care if he never boarded another train in his life.

So Bone did the only thing that felt right. He let the New Orleans boy be, and he sent his old friend's corpse out to Louisiana.

The tale was considered quite a lark around town, but the last laugh was on Bone. When he himself died some years later, down and out and waiting for a money order in the Fort Ogden Depot, his remains were placed in an unmarked grave in the Joshua Creek Cemetery. Thirty years on, some of his old friends decided to do him a good turn and finally inscribe him a nice tombstone.

The only problem was they placed it on the wrong grave. After a few days, two of his relatives, Smoot and Mayo Johnson, crept into the cemetery and corrected the error.

On second thought, maybe that means ol' Bone had the last laugh on all of us.

Lord knows it wouldn't have been the first time.

## ADDISON MIZNER: SEPARATING FACT FROM FICTION

Addison Mizner (1872–1933) was the California-born visionary behind the Mediterranean- and Spanish Colonial Revival–style architecture of Boca Raton most prominently displayed in the world-famous Boca Raton Resort & Club. Mizner was larger than life, so tall tales about him are bound to be whoppers. Thanks to Susan Gillis, curator of the Boca Raton Historical Society and Museum, here are a few:

According to popular belief, Mizner, who lacked any architectural education and had a poor professional reputation, "invented" Boca Raton. He painted his famous Cloister Inn (which became the Resort & Club) pink because the hue reflected the light of dawn. Perhaps because he was in such a hurry to get the inn finished, the columns lining the "cloister" of the inn, a loggia fronting Lake Boca Raton, were installed upside down. What's more, his ten original model homes for the subdivision Old Floresta mysteriously lacked kitchens.

Those are the stories. Here is the truth: Mizner, in fact, apprenticed as an architect rather than enrolling in a school program, a common practice at the time. He was widely respected by his colleagues. The hotel's third owners painted it pink, not him. The columns aren't upside down at all; that's the Gothic style. Finally, Boca Raton was settled by Europeans by 1895, long before Mizner arrived. And just for the record: all his homes had kitchens.

Which isn't to say he wasn't in a hurry to finish. In fact, his engineer had to remind him that he needed floor plans before he could get to work.

Addison Mizner and friend. *Boca Raton Historical Society and Museum.*

## AN OCALA LEGEND: THE BRICK CITY FIRE

Every year at Thanksgiving time, the downtown district of Ocala is ablaze with thousands of shimmering white lights, making it almost appear as if the Marion County city were actually on fire. The event, known as Light Up Ocala, is a fitting testament to the events of Thanksgiving Day 1883, when the city did, in fact, nearly burn to the ground. Historians agree that the Ocala that emerged from the ashes learned its lesson: buildings were no longer made of wood, and Ocala at last got its own fire brigade. What folks can't quite agree on, however, are the exact circumstances surrounding the fire. And how many tourists and newcomers know why so many local business names begin with the words "Brick City"?

It was a cool, sunny Thanksgiving morning, and the word around Captain Samuel Agnew's brand-new Palace Hotel was that a celebrity was scheduled to arrive in Ocala for the opening ceremonies that weekend. No one knew quite who it was, but the rumors swirled. After all, this was a fine hotel in the midst of Central Florida's most prosperous community—less than forty years old and already one of the largest in the state. Maybe former president Grant would pay a return visit! The manager pressed

Deland firefighters at the 1884 State Fire Department Contests in Ocala, which at the time had no fire department. *State Archives of Florida.*

everybody into service polishing and sweeping and giving the windowsills the white glove test. The new, sixty-five-room hotel had to outshine its biggest competitor, the Ocala House.

At the time, the city, which had recently climbed out of a deep economic hole, still looked like little more than a dusty frontier town, with all the loose living that accompanied it. There was no dearth of bars, and the wooden buildings and unpaved streets of downtown—which, along with a few odd homes, included the newspaper office, a barber and blacksmith shop, stables and outhouses—did not exactly invite acclaim. But all this had started to change, with the railroad coming in to take the area's ample produce and livestock to larger markets. And now there would be the Palace. It was, to be sure, the dawn of a new era.

No one knew who first sounded the alarm about the smoke wafting from the upper stories of the Benjamin Company Store, at the corner of Main and Ocklawaha. Some say clerks who were sleeping on the second floor knocked down an oil lamp and called out for help. In any event, some say the Methodist church bells began to ring at 5:00 a.m. Or perhaps it was someone in the enormous crowd waiting at the station to spend the holiday in the country who spotted the smoke.

The question was, who was there to help put out the blaze? Certainly not the local fire department. In their attempts to curb costs, the city fathers hadn't bothered to fund one. Instead, citizens hastily drew water from a single horse trough; its pump was located about a quarter mile from the flames. What with the wind and the lack of proper equipment, the situation quickly became catastrophic. When the smoke cleared, five city blocks were destroyed, with damages to the tune of $350,000.

With a can-do spirit and pockets full of cash, the town leaders got to work rebuilding the downtown, this time with plenty of brick, steel and granite instead of wood, by no means an inexpensive proposition. Next they began the task of creating a fire department by issuing bonds, which took another four years.

By the end of the century, the town square was a modern wonder to behold, and Ocala was known far and wide as the "Brick City." But the Palace Hotel never did get to hold that ceremony.

## How Orlando Got Its Name

History is a funny thing. Without solid documentation, it's next to impossible to figure out something as simple as how a major U.S. city got its name. On the other hand, maybe folks didn't know it back then, either. There could have been several good reasons to choose the same name, and the best story might have just stuck.

Some researchers point out that a prominent landowner named Orlando J. Rees lived in the vicinity of the current Central Florida city in the 1830s. Others say a "Mr. Orlando" was killed in the area while making his way to Tampa, and he was buried where he fell. Then there's the story of the influential judge who apparently was such a Shakespeare fan that he promoted the name Orlando for the city after a character in the bard's comedy *As You Like It*. (Proponents of this theory point to a main street through the heart of the city named Rosalind, the name of the character married to Orlando in the play. Coincidence?)

One of the best-known legends is included here, but questions still arise as to the soldier's last name. Was it Reeves? Was it Jennings? And why are neither of these names listed on the War Department's roster of deaths during the Seminole Wars?

Not that it really matters much. After all, plenty of folks these days simply think of the city as "Mickey's Town."

In 1835, the Second Seminole War was just beginning, and forts were springing up throughout the region to drive the natives off their lands and recapture the runaway slaves who had sought refuge with them. One such fort, Gatlin, overlooked three lakes in what was to become a decade later Central Florida. The fort gave soldiers not only an excellent view of the territory but also exceptional mobility.

Sometime in the fall of that year, a U.S. soldier named Orlando Reeves was tracking Seminoles with his men in swampland not far from the fort. When night fell, the men made camp, and Reeves drew guard duty.

Reeves was a fine, upstanding young man who took his responsibilities seriously. For many hours, he paced back and forth at his post, fighting to stay awake and catch sight of movement, light or anything at all that would signify a threat to the fort and, thus, his brothers in arms.

Just before dawn, he was scanning the horizon when he thought he saw what he had taken for a tree trunk move a few inches to the right. He stood

The fabulous Orlando skyline. *Miosotis Jade, Wikimedia Commons.*

stock still, waiting, hardly daring to draw breath. Sure enough, after several minutes, he sighted another flicker of movement in the same spot. He hesitated not an instant, even though he must have known that sounding the alarm would cost him his life.

"Indians!"

That was the last word Orlando Reeves ever spoke. An arrow pierced his heart not a second later, and several more surrounded it. He fell to the ground, with his musket clattering alongside him.

The soldiers responded instantly. Still, it took some time for the natives to retreat. After the bloody battle, Orlando Reeves's comrades carried his body back inside the fort, where it was prepared for burial. The following day, they selected a nice patch of land near a spring, and for years to come, the spot was known as Orlando's Grave.

With the birth of the state of Florida in 1845, Mosquito County, where the fort was located, was renamed Orange County, and a name for the county seat was required. The town fathers were leaning toward Gatlin, but there were enough towns named after forts already.

"We need a strong name," one man said.

"A name that spells freedom," suggested another.

"Let's name it after that soldier fella gave his life to save the fort," another one suggested. "What was his name again?"

All agreed that the name Orlando had a lovely ring to it. It was one of the few decisions the men didn't have to fight very hard to agree on.

## JUAN ORTIZ AND ULELE: A DeSoto County Legend

Can there ever be too many Pocahontas stories? There are at least two in Florida, and let's not forget the better-known tale of John Smith in Virginia, which supposedly occurred seven or eight decades later— although historians believe that Smith modeled his story on that of Juan Ortiz long after the demise of the native woman in question.

The attraction of the trope is obvious: exotic daughter of the enemy falls for, and rescues, white male. But beyond that, there is, perhaps, a more political implication to our twenty-first-century sensibilities. How bad could the European invaders have been, the stories suggest, if the native daughters begged to save their lives?

At the mouth of the Little Manatee River in the vicinity of Tampa Bay was a native village named Uzita. In that village lived Ulele, a Tocobaga princess, with her father, Hirrihiqua, the chief of the tribe.

When the Spanish conquistador Panfilo de Narvaez arrived with his men in 1528, he wasted no time establishing his well-deserved reputation for cruelty. Demanding to be introduced to the chief, one of his first acts was to take out his machete and cut off Hirrihiqua's nose. In the ensuing chaos, he ordered his soldiers to feed the man's mother to the company's dogs before leaving the village.

Little wonder that the chief made it known to his warriors that he would do anything to exact revenge on the Spanish. His hatred grew like a sickness in his belly, until he could think of little else.

Several of Narvaez's men did not go ashore when the others were terrorizing the natives, however. One of these was an eighteen-year-old son of a nobleman whose name was Juan Ortiz. Ortiz's job, along with a few others, was to take the boat back to their base in Cuba for supplies. He stayed on the island for some time, doing whatever work was needed and enjoying a moderately peaceful life. Ortiz could not have been more different than his captain. He had signed on to the ship for the adventure, yes. But not for the bloodshed.

Then one day, Ortiz was summoned, along with a few dozen from the ship, to return to Florida. It seemed that Narvaez's wife, who had not heard from her husband in many months, was worried that he was in danger, and the captain wanted to reassure her.

When he heard that he was chosen for the expedition, the young man shrugged. It was nice in Cuba; he had heard that it was also nice in Florida. As long as he got paid and didn't have to work too hard, he would go wherever and do whatever he was asked.

As the ship entered Tampa Bay and approached the spot where they had laid anchor before, the crew spotted a small vessel sailing toward them. In it were several natives, and the Spanish wasted no time in taking them prisoner. Then they drew near the shore and saw a strange sight on the beach. It appeared to be a stick propped in the sand, with a note attached. Ortiz and three others got out to investigate.

As if out of nowhere, dozens of warriors surrounded them and took them to their chief. Sentence and execution were swift for the three older men. But when it came to Ortiz, the chief hesitated.

"This one reminds me of his chief," he said, referring to Narvaez. "This one I shall take special pleasure in killing." To the young man's horror, a sort of grill was quickly set up, and he was tied to the surface above the red-hot coals.

At the sound of the young man's screams, a number of horrified villagers came forward to beg the chief for mercy. Among them was his daughter.

"I know you don't want him here," she cried when she reached her father, "but that doesn't mean you have to show the cruelty that his people did to us. Let us send him to the village of my betrothed. Mococo will know what to do with him."

Perhaps because he loved his daughter, perhaps because he had already killed three men, the chief did as she asked. So it was that Juan Ortiz lived with Mococo's people for a dozen years, nearly forgetting Spanish in the process of learning the native language.

One day, he was told that scouts had spotted a Spanish cavalry patrol in the area, and he was free to rejoin his people. But when he rushed out to them, he was attacked by gunfire. At the last minute, he recalled a bit of a Spanish prayer.

"*Padre nuestro que estas en los cielos!*" he screamed. "Our father who art in heaven!"

At the sound of the prayer, the shots were silenced. Ortiz slowly approached the soldiers and, in broken Spanish, explained his plight. He was taken on board to meet the expedition leader, Hernando de Soto, who had succeeded Narvaez as the man in charge of Florida. Ortiz served as interpreter, but it was a sorrowful existence. He was now carrying out the orders of a man at least as brutal as Narvaez. The difference was that in the intervening years, he had come to regard the Tocobaga as his people. His heart split in two between his new culture and his old, the man came to regard his every deed for de Soto as torture.

It is said that the site of the Pinellas Point Temple Mound in Saint Petersburg is the spot where Ulele begged her father for Ortiz's life. There were times in the ensuing years when he wasn't all that sure he was grateful to her.

## CHIEF OSCEOLA: A SEMINOLE WARRIOR

The legends surrounding the life and death of the great Seminole chief Osceola illustrate the important distinction between folk narrative and historical record. The man for whom, among other things, a county, school and roads were named and at least one statue stands may have been born in North Carolina or Alabama. He may or may not have made a violent action when ordered to sign a treaty with the U.S. government. But what we take away from his story is, one could argue, more important than the historical record. Osceola was a proud, brave man who would not kowtow to the enemy. And that makes him a role model for all of us, whatever our background and whatever the details.

Fort Moultrie National Park sits on Sullivan's Island, South Carolina, just a short distance from Charleston, the city the fort was built to protect during the Revolutionary War. Years later, a great Seminole chief was buried on the site. The marker reads, "Osceola, Patriot and Warrior, died at Fort Moultrie, January 30, 1838." To understand how this native warrior got a military burial in a United States fort, we must begin, as they say, at the beginning.

In 1804, a son was born to Polly Coppinger, from the Creek (or Muskogee, as they called themselves) tribe, and William Powell, a Scots-Irish trader, in a Creek village in Alabama called Talisi. Named after his absent father, the child was known as Billy.

By 1814, Polly and Billy were pushed out of their lands south to Florida, along with others from their tribe. Billy was a young man living with his mother when one of the tribal elders summoned him.

"You are a good boy," the elder said, "and you will soon be an adult. We have watched you since you arrived here, and you carry yourself with dignity and bring honor to everything you do. We are proud to call you once of us."

Billy bowed his head and remained silent, curious to find out what the man had in mind for him. Since arriving in Florida, he had felt a strange disconnect between his Creek heritage and that of his English father. Where was he? What was he? How did it happen that the Americans who now inhabited his tribal lands hated both of his people, the British they had fought against in the past and the Creek they were destroying now?

The old man interrupted his thoughts. "You have been William Powell long enough. We have decided it is time for you to carry a name that reflects the other part of your heritage. The part that the white man is persecuting you for. The part for which you should be most proud."

"I have waited for this for quite some time," the young boy said. "What have you chosen for me?"

"Uhsee-yahola," the elder replied solemnly. "For our ceremonial drink *uhsee*, because you are a man of spirit, and *yahola*, the 'shouter,' because you are a man of action. You have earned a mighty name, Uhsee-yahola, and you will live up to it and make us proud in these terrible days."

"I give you my word," he said.

"As well you should. We will make it official at this year's Green Corn Ceremony, in July. Then you will raise the conch shell and drink the black drink for which you are named. It will make you feel sick, but it will cleanse and transform you.

"With a name like that," the old man continued, "you will be a great leader of our people. And with your dual heritage, you will be a bridge between one side and the other."

Billy knew the meeting was over, but he sat just a moment longer, savoring the moment. A leader of his people, he thought. And he knew just what he would lead his people to do. Stand up to the Americans!

By 1821, when the United States acquired Florida from the Spanish, the pressure on native peoples throughout the South to leave their lands was building. Then, with the reluctant signing of their first treaty two years later, the tribes became residents of the four-million-acre reservation in Central

Florida. Some told themselves they were lucky to be alive; others said they wished they were dead.

One part of the treaty concerned the return of escaped African slaves to the government, which would, in turn, return them to their owners. Many of these men and women had joined the native peoples, and although there were some among the tribes who were glad to give them up, Osceola did not agree. In fact, his wife was a former slave.

When the two were joined in marriage, she had told him, "You must defend my people as you do your own. You must not help the Americans uphold slavery."

"I give you my word," he said.

Another treaty, in 1832, was designed to send the Seminole people—the name for the tribes in Florida—out west of the Mississippi.

By that time, Osceola had indeed become a leader of his people. He lived near present-day Ocala, and he was in the room when the chiefs were signing. One by one, some steeling themselves to hold back tears, they made their marks on the paper. When the document came to him along with the quill and ink, he pulled out his knife and stabbed a hole in the page. A scuffle ensued, but Osceola was soon released, and the hole served as his mark.

And so the expulsions and the fighting and the deaths waged on. When some of the tribal leaders refused to do what they were told, the U.S. military deposed them from their positions. Soon, no native was allowed to carry a gun.

Despite his fury at the fate of his people, Osceola maintained good relationships with a few of the government officials. One of them in particular, the U.S. Indian agent Wiley Thompson, he had come to think of as almost a friend.

"Wiley," he said one day, sitting down in the white man's office not long after the ban on weapons had been announced. "You are treating my people no better than slaves. We are the enemy of the Americans, but we are free men."

"You are hardly free men," the agent replied. "But even if I could reverse the ban, I wouldn't. Why would I want to arm the very people who are rebelling against us?"

"Let me hold onto my rifle," Osceola said. "I will not use it against a white man. But you have already taken my lands. At least leave me my manhood."

Thompson fingered the inkwell on his desk for a long minute. Then he sighed.

"This is probably the stupidest move I've ever made," he said. "But believe it or not, I hate this situation as much as you do. Go on, keep your weapon."

It wasn't long before the two were at odds, however, and Thompson himself ordered Osceola to be locked up in Fort King. When he regained his freedom, Osceola could not forgive the humiliation. Just after the white man's Christmas, in 1835, he led an attack. He was not sorry to learn that Wiley Thompson was one of the first casualties.

Not two years later, Osceola decided that his people had suffered enough, and he saw no hope for them. He raised the white flag of truce in his camp and awaited the American general. But against all rules of engagement, he and his men were captured and imprisoned at Fort Marion in St. Augustine.

Broken at last, Osceola sat in his cell, refusing food and talking to no one.

One night, he heard whispering. "Osceola," the voice said. "You must come with us. We leave tonight!"

He had already heard the rumors of escape, but he had had enough of the fight. He turned his head to the wall and willed himself to sleep.

Following the daring escape, the Americans moved many of the captives to Fort Moultrie, in the belief that the island fort would be more secure.

What they weren't counting on was popular opinion. Criticism was rampant, both in Congress and in the press. How could a man like Osceola, who had only wished to make peace, be imprisoned?

Before those in power could decide what to do with him, the great man fell ill in the damp fort. By the time he died on January 30, 1838, he had led five successful attacks against his enemies and was a hero to his people.

After all, he had given his word.


## PONCE DE LEON AND THE FOUNTAIN OF YOUTH

Stop the presses: the Fountain of Youth has been found! It is located in a well near the road leading to the airport in Bimini, and in Florida north of Deland, and in Holmes County, and in Safety Harbor, and in Silver Springs and, of course, at 11 Magnolia Avenue, St. Augustine, site of Ponce de Leon's Fountain of Youth Archaeological Park. While we're at it, we might also count the West Palm Beach International Airport, where seniors who board flights on wheelchairs in New York run on two strong legs upon arrival in order to catch their rides. (Down here we call these wonders of recuperation "miracle flights.")

Ponce de Leon's search for the Fountain of Youth is the stuff of legend. *Library of Congress.*

Actually, the scoop isn't that there are numerous Fountains of Youth, the apparent goal of Spanish explorer Juan Ponce de Leon when he arrived in St. Augustine in 1513. (We'll skip the point that he may have in fact arrived first about 140 miles south, around Melbourne.) The surprise, to many, is that he was never looking for the alleged fountain in the first place.

Yes, the fact that Florida owes its discovery by Europeans to a native myth is, in fact, a Spanish legend.

Ponce de Leon was undoubtedly aware of the numerous tales that existed since at least the time of Alexander the Great, perhaps originating among indigenous peoples of the Caribbean, about the existence of a fountain with remarkable powers in the New World. But in sixteenth-century Spain, such stories were largely considered a load of hooey. No, it was gold and land that Ponce de Leon was seeking for Spain—as well as a fair bit of glory for himself.

The reputation-tarnishing story circulated after the explorer's death and was created by a political enemy in Spain, who just happened to be the court chronicler.

That's how rumors get started.

## THE DUCHESS AND THE INN: A ROYAL VISIT TO INDIANTOWN

Today, Indiantown is a sleepy little hamlet with a population of about six thousand. The small downtown strip, Warfield Boulevard, is dotted with small businesses and a few fast-food joints. On my visit to the area, the Seminole Inn, by far the most interesting spot on the block, served up tasty fried green tomatoes and the "best fried chicken in the South" to the few who stopped by on a lazy Saturday afternoon. But for a short period in the 1920s, the former Seminole trading post located just thirty miles northwest of Palm Beach was poised to become a major Florida transportation hub. What it didn't count on was two storms, one of which was a connection to a woman destined to be at the very center of a royal scandal.

Solomon Davies Warfield looked up from his drink and smiled at the young matron across the table, but she was too busy attending to her guests to notice. He had known his niece all her life and had supported her and her mother since her father, his youngest brother, died soon after the child's birth. Now thirty, Bessie Wallis, who these days was known as simply Wallis, had separated from her husband after an indiscretion halfway around the world and was, as far as he could make out, at loose ends. Knowing his niece to be very good in social situations, Warfield had prevailed upon her to join him down in rural Florida.

The year was 1926, and the Baltimore banker and railroad executive was facing one of the greatest challenges of his long, full life. Two years

Edward and Wallis, the Duke and Duchess of Windsor. *Media Museum at Flickrs Commons.*

earlier, he had extended his Seaboard Air Line Railway linking east and west Florida an additional two-hundred-plus miles from Coleman, in the center of the state, southeast to West Palm Beach. Just about thirty-five miles away, Indiantown was a stop on the line and the site of his company's southern headquarters.

The state was in the middle of an extraordinary land boom, and S. Davies Warfield had made sure to capitalize on it. Having decided to leave a legacy by making little Indiantown a model city, he hired a raft of fancy big-city experts to design streets, housing, even a school. Such a town required an elegant hotel, and so he had built one. His jewel. His Seminole Inn. Set to open tonight.

He planned or signed off on every detail. The double French doors marking the entrance. The open fireplace and winding staircases. The solid brass wall fixtures and bronze chandeliers. Warfield had carefully selected and happily purchased everything from the pecky cypress ceilings to the hardwood floors.

To top off the effect, he had invited his niece to serve as hostess for the grand opening of the inn. Not exactly a beauty, Wallis nonetheless exuded a remarkable sense of style, with those violet-blue eyes and her impeccable taste in clothing. A bachelor in late middle age, Warfield liked the idea of having a fashionable, quick-witted young woman on his arm when he ushered in the swells.

True to form, she carried out her duties like a pro, greeting guests young and old, wealthy and powerful, with poise and equanimity. He had done well by sending her to that fancy school in Maryland, he reflected. Now if she could only settle down and stay out of trouble, he could rest easy about her. There was some talk about another man while she was still married in China and an unwanted pregnancy. Not liking to think about it, he took his last swallow of brandy and held up the snifter to a passing waitress for a refill.

So much opportunity for each of them, he thought. Listening to his dinner guest with half an ear, he kept his eye on Wallis and wondered what the future would bring for himself and his niece. He had done all he could for them both; now it was up to fate to decide the rest.

Months passed, and fate intervened, with a nasty hurricane that marked the beginning of the end of the Florida land boom. The old man died the following year, and Wallis remarried two years later. Not long after that, she met and fell in love with the Prince of Wales, the future King Edward VIII. The ensuing affair and his abdication of the throne to marry her reverberated around the world.

That wasn't quite the end of Indiantown's brush with fame, however. In 1970, the train stopped in Indiantown just so that Wallis Simpson, by then known as the Duchess of Windsor, could visit the Seminole Inn once again.

And in 1994, Hollywood royalty in the person of local boy Burt Reynolds shot some of his 1994 TV movie *The Man from Left Field* on the premises.

In between, the Duke and Duchess of Windsor's home in Paris became well known in society circles for its lavish parties. Wallis served as the gracious hostess, much as she had done years before at her uncle's famous Seminole Inn, when there was nothing but promise in the air for little Indiantown.

## "I've Got Some Swampland in Florida to Sell You!"

Huge swaths of the Everglades have been successfully—albeit to the detriment of the environment—drained to create fine communities in many areas of the state. Nevertheless, the expression "I've got some swampland in Florida to sell you" does not tend to evoke images of Walt Disney's empire in the Kissimmee/Orlando area. In fact, the only phrase more popular for gulling a person ripe for scamming is, "You wanna buy the Brooklyn Bridge?"

The height of the Florida land scams associated with such names as Charles Ponzi (Jacksonville), the Rosen brothers' Gulf American Land Corporation (Cape Coral, Lake Wales, Golden Gate) and Lee Ratner and Gerald Gould (Lehigh Acres) took place in the 1920s through the 1960s. But the con is certainly still being practiced somewhere. Eager, greedy investors, spurred on by lavish national advertising campaigns and, at times,

Ohio resident Elsie Keller at Lee County subdivision Lehigh Acres, 1963. *State Archives of Florida/Keller.*

booths in New York City railroad stations, purchased property for as little as 10 percent down—sight unseen. And few people asked questions. At one time, the former secretary of state and early twentieth-century presidential candidate William Jennings Bryan even got into the land scam act.

Unfortunately, far more people suffered than simply the unwitting buyers. Two years after the real estate bubble burst in 1926, partly as a result of two killer hurricanes, $1 billion in Florida property could be had for a measly $143 million. Even today, undeveloped and underdeveloped property is both a blight on the landscape and a drain on communities.

But while the booms lasted, they sure made for terrific stories.

## TATE'S HELL STATE FOREST: A CARABELLE LEGEND

*Oh listen, good people*
*A story I'll tell*
*Of a great swamp in Florida*
*A place called Tate's Hell.*
—*Will McLean*

A number of people have recorded Will McLean's version of the grisly legend of one man's fight against nature, including his fellow Florida folk singer (and storyteller) Bob Patterson, who made it the first cut on his album *Remember*. What exactly did befall a probably fictional Sumatra, Florida rancher we will never know. But one thing is for certain: it was pretty awful. To this day, some locals say that on certain nights, a ghostly light dances through the state forest known as Tate's Hell. But it's hard to believe that even the ghost of Cebe Tate would ever venture back into those woods of his own free will.

First, a bit of background: the Homestead Act of 1862 encouraged many hardy individuals throughout the nation to try their hand at the pioneer life. Settlers received 160 acres of public land in exchange for a small fee and a big catch: five years of continuous residence on the site.

By 1875, a homesteader named Cebe Tate had staked his claim in the Florida Panhandle, in a piece of land in Sumatra, less than thirty miles from

Carabelle on the Gulf of Mexico. He built himself a house and a barn, invested in some cows and horses and figured he had it made.

But like many homesteaders, Tate had a problem: panthers. One morning, after finding several cow carcasses on his property, he decided he'd finally had enough. He gathered up his shotgun and his two best hunting dogs and took to the woods.

After a few hours of aimless wandering, the dogs seemed to pick up a scent. They flew off with Cebe in the rear, but he soon lost them in the underbrush. As if that weren't bad enough, when he stopped to get a drink of water at a stream, he was bitten by a snake. Things went from bad to worse when he reached for his gun and realized he'd somehow managed to drop it along the way.

It didn't take long for Tate to lose his sense of direction. For seven days and nights he roamed the ancient trees and ominous swampland, more often than not dazed with hunger and heat, forced to live on nothing but roots and muddy water. To make matters worse, the mosquitoes swarmed around him until every inch of his body was bitten.

Just when he became certain he was going to die in that awful place, Cebe Tate spotted an opening in the trees and, to his shock and delight, came face to face with two hunters. To his eyes, they looked like gods. To theirs, the emaciated man, filthy and ragged, looked like a ghost. Far from the hale and hearty forty-five-year-old pioneer who had entered the woods, he had turned, in just a week, white-haired and frail.

"Are you okay, friend?" one of them asked as Tate stepped into the clearing.

"You look like you've been in there a month," the other said. "You know where you are? This here is Carabelle."

He didn't utter a word, just stared at the two as if not believing they were real.

"What's your name, friend?" the first hunter persisted. "Where did you come from?"

It took a few minutes for the dazed man to form the words, but when he did, they were memorable.

"My name is Cebe Tate," he said. "And I come from hell."

## JULIA TUTTLE'S ORANGE BLOSSOMS

When the infamous Great Freeze descended on Florida in two separate frosts during the winter of 1894–95, the state's citrus growers, who at the time were

For Julia Tuttle, one orange blossom was worth a thousand words. *Library of Congress.*

selling five million boxes of fruit a year, were caught totally unprepared. That December, for the first time in a century, thermometers in Orlando registered a mere eighteen degrees Fahrenheit, and in February, West Palm residents endured record-breaking temperatures as low as twenty-seven. The citrus crop, which depended on warm weather, was decimated.

Whole towns, such as Earnestville, about forty miles north of Tampa, died along with their crops, while others that had managed to elude the frosts, such as Keystone Lake (cleverly renamed Frostproof), flourished. Seemingly overnight, the Florida citrus industry changed forever, as wary growers either got out of the business altogether or relocated as far south as possible.

That much of the following story is historically accurate. The truth behind the famous tale of how the Great Freeze led to the extension of the Florida East Coast Railway, however, is a little murkier. And yet, like most legends, it has four elements of a great story: first, a man, a woman—and an against-all-odds obsession. And then, for good measure, there is that magnificent image of orange blossoms.

Julia Tuttle put down the letter she was reading, took off her glasses and sighed. It was early March 1895, and a friend in Orlando had just written to her about the terrible effects of the winter freeze. She had long since received similar news from acquaintances in Pasco County. Even south of

Tampa, the citrus had frozen on the tree branches and the bark had peeled off the trunks. It was a disaster not only for the growers but also for the entire state, as land values that were already dismal couldn't stand much more decline. It was worse than a disaster, she felt. It was a tragedy.

Mrs. Tuttle knew about tragedy. Her husband had died nine years before, and he had left her, to her shock, penniless. But she was a smart, strong woman, just thirty-seven years of age at the time, and she had known how to pull herself together and get things done. She simply took boarders into her Cleveland home to pay the bills. And she would have probably still been doing that if her father hadn't died, as well.

Now, she and her children were living in her father's big house on several hundred acres of land along the Miami River, with a spectacular view of both the river and Biscayne Bay. The place had once served as army barracks and, before that, slave quarters. Now, after months of work, it was to her eyes the most beautiful home in the world.

Tuttle had fallen in love with the area the moment she set eyes on it, twenty years before, when she first visited. What she had never been able to understand was why the Florida railroad magnates—Mr. Plant on the west coast and Mr. Flagler, whose tracks stopped at West Palm Beach, on the east—didn't seem to see the area's potential as she did. She had even met Henry Flagler, a fellow Clevelander, in their hometown, and she had beseeched him to come visit her and experience this paradise-on-earth for himself. If he would just spend an hour on Biscayne Bay, she felt sure, he wouldn't hesitate to extend his railroad all the way south. But somehow he had never found the time.

Now with this freeze, she thought, we'll be lucky to get him to maintain the tracks he's already built. Shaking her head, she reached for an orange.

Good thing we still have plenty of citrus down here, she thought. I always eat when I'm upset.

And just like that, she had another thought. The vast majority of the state's crop was devastated, she knew, but not south of her and not less than a dozen miles north. If Henry Flagler wanted to ensure the continued growth of the tourism and citrus industries in Florida—thus justifying the massive expense of his railroad—then he would simply have to extend the tracks!

She jumped up and called for her overseer.

"I want you to go out to the groves," she told the man. "Here." She reached into a nearby cupboard for a big wicker basket. "And fill this with orange blossoms."

The man gave her a puzzled look. "Just blossoms? No fruit, ma'am?"

"Just blossoms," she said. "And please hurry!"

She dressed quickly and carried the basket of blossoms to the post office herself. At the same time, she sent a telegram to Henry Flagler. It read: "Region around shores of Biscayne Bay untouched by freezes. Please come see for yourself."

On her way back home, she couldn't help smiling. This one-horse town won't be so small for long, she thought. It's going to be a metropolis.

Instead of making the trip himself, however, Flagler sent down two men who worked for him in Palm Beach. They returned to their boss with all the oranges, grapefruit and other produce they could carry.

The next day, Tuttle received a cable from the railroad magnate. "Madam," it said simply, "what is it that you propose?"

Julia Tuttle's plan, which came to pass within a year, was simple: extend the tracks down to Biscayne Bay. Build a big hotel for the tourists. In exchange, she would give him 50 acres of her land, plus half of the 640 acres she owned north of the river. Her neighbor William Brickell, also a fellow Clevelander, incidentally, agreed to provide half of his own land south of the river.

In mid-April 1896, the first Florida East Coast train arrived at Biscayne Bay, with the railroad tycoon Henry Flagler on board. It was followed, two days later, by the first regular passenger train.

The city of Miami was incorporated three months after that, on July 28, 1896. Population: a paltry three hundred.

For Julia Tuttle, widely hailed today as the mother of Miami, it was a great start.

## MILLY FRANCIS: THE WAKULLA POCAHONTAS

Situated in the Edward Ball Wakulla Springs State Park about fifteen miles south of Tallahassee, Wakulla Springs is the world's largest and deepest body of water of its kind. It flows into the ten-mile-long Wakulla River, which eventually lends its waters to the St. Marks River, just three miles from the Gulf. At least as early as twenty thousand years ago, in the Paleo period, native peoples enjoyed the pristine beauty of the area.

History tells us that a fifteen-year-old Creek girl named Milly Francis really did save the life of a U.S. militiaman on the banks of the Wakulla River, and she really was called Pocahontas in the popular press. She went on to marry a Creek warrior who later died, after which she suffered the infamous Trail of Tears and was living in poverty in what became Oklahoma, until she was rediscovered and, after two years of deliberation, voted a nice pension and medal from the government.

Predictably, some variants of the legend, like this one, are a lot more romantic.

Milly's father was a great man. She had known this as long as she'd known her own name. Called the Prophet Francis, or Hillis Hadjo, he was a Creek leader, and he hated the tribe's assimilationists and collaborators with the white man nearly as much as he hated the Europeans and Americans who forced his people out of their villages. Maybe more.

By the spring of 1818, General Andrew Jackson's four thousand troops, half of whom were Creek themselves, had invaded Florida, forcing the native peoples east of the Suwannee River. Known as the First Seminole War out of three, this was not the first provocation against natives in the Southeast, and it would certainly not be the last. Years earlier, Hadjo had been a Red Stick resistance fighter, intractable against the white oppressors, but that had only bought his people a little time. Now, war was all around them, and their water paradise, once so peaceful and protective, had become a bloody battlefield.

Milly Francis was just fifteen, pretty and imbued from birth with a life force that everyone who knew her said would either serve her well or bring her shame. She shrugged off the comments. She wanted to be involved in important events, like her father. She wanted to do the right thing. How she did it was not so important.

Born in Alabama, she had come south as a child with her mother and little sister when her people were pushed in that direction by the invaders. Florida was so different from home—so much coastline, so much water. The Wakulla River was dark and mysterious, but she had taken to it right away, spending long afternoons lounging on its banks, waiting for her father to return from his diplomatic mission in England and dreaming about the brave and handsome warrior she would one day marry.

She knew what had happened at Fort Gadsden, of course. Some Creeks had helped the Americans stage a bloody massacre of Seminole and Choctaw and African slaves there just two years before, when the Fourth Infantry invaded. By the time her father had returned from Europe, he was back in the thick of battle. Now, the white general Andrew Jackson was occupying the fort on the Apalachicola River. What would happen to her father, and her people, she hated to think.

As she lay on the riverbank, the comforting songs of the birds in the surrounding trees were suddenly drowned out by a cacophony of war whoops and hurried footsteps. She jumped up and followed the sound. To her shock, she saw a white soldier, not much older than she, skinny and fresh-faced and shaking with fear from the gray wool shoulders of his uniform to his battered shoes, fighting in vain to escape the clutches of her father's two most trusted warriors.

An interpreter was quickly summoned, and it was discovered that the young man was named Duncan McCrimmon and that he was a private, the lowest of the low, from a small city in Georgia called Milledgeville.

Standing back from the crowd, Milly missed not a word or a gesture of the ensuing discussion. She had seen Union soldiers, of course, but they were mostly screaming, shooting and galloping by on horseback. Never had she seen one so scared or so close. Or so young. And what were the warriors holding up? Why, it looked like a fishing rod! The soldier was probably trying to feed himself to keep from starving!

Her father murmured something to his men and followed them as they dragged the soldier away. Soon after, the others dispersed, laughing and pointing. Everyone left but Milly. She stood as if rooted to the spot, unable to take a step. She knew what would happen to the young man if no one intervened. She knew he had probably killed many of her people. But something was terribly wrong.

"Father?" she asked, forcing herself to run up to her father. "Could I speak with you?"

"What is it, little one?" he asked, falling back from his men. "We are executing the prisoner, so I must be quick."

"Why do you have to do that, Father?" she asked, tears brimming in her eyes. "It's one thing to shoot the enemy in battle, but why do we do that to him just because he went fishing?"

"My dear," he said. His eyes were kind but his mouth set. "I am a warrior and a leader of our people. If I do not give the order to kill him, he will kill many more of us. Is that what you want?"

"I just think we should be fair," she said, her head held high but her chin quivering. "The man was not harming us when he was captured."

The prophet sighed. "You know our way," he said at last. "His life belongs to the warrior who found him. If you must, go to him and ask for his life."

When Milly found the others, they had already stripped Duncan McCrimmon and tied him to a tree. She saw the sharp ribs pressing out against his skin and looked away. The warriors who had brought him to her father were loading the rifles they had taken long before from other white men.

Fearless, Milly ran up to them. As she did so, she tried to avoid staring at the soldier, who was, despite the greater fear of death, trying to hide his nakedness. She could not avoid his eyes, however, which followed her every movement, dark with desperation.

"Please," she said, bowing before the eldest of the warriors. "May I speak to you?"

The warrior nodded, still looking down at his gun.

"Please spare the life of this young man," she said. At the sound of her words, a hush fell over the assembled men.

The warrior looked up. "And why should I? You know that my sister has been killed in this bloody war. It is my turn, the tribe's turn, for revenge."

"Your sister will be dead whether or not you take the life of this young man," she said quietly. "And think. Maybe he will return to his people and tell them that we are just and merciful."

The oldest warrior hesitated and then looked at the others.

"Or else he will tell them we are weak." He sighed and shook his head. "And what does your father say about this?" he asked, his eyes still on the other men.

"He says the matter is in your hands and yours alone."

Maybe the warrior was thinking that the girl was so young and so pretty. Maybe he was thinking that the chief would be kindly disposed to him if he did what the girl wanted.

He shrugged. "I can do this for you," he said, dropping his rifle and motioning to the others to do the same. "We will not kill this man if he shaves his head and adopts our dress."

She turned to the weeping soldier, still bound to the tree. He made a mewling sound, like a cat, and nodded.

Days later, Duncan McCrimmon was returned to the Spanish garrison and traded for several gallons of rum. Not many weeks afterward, General Jackson and his men took over the fort, and the young man went back to his people.

It is said that the rescued private proposed to Milly through an interpreter.

When the young girl got the message, she smiled. Was this, in fact, the warrior she had dreamed of, what seemed an eternity ago? Her father's daughter, she would never abandon her community. She could only help lead them. By marrying this young man, she might become a bridge between her people and his. Together, they might help put an end to the fighting. And besides, she had also fallen in love with him.

And so she happily accepted.

## THE LIFE AND DEATH OF ED WATSON: AN EVERGLADES LEGEND

The life and death of Edgar "Bloody" Watson were the raw material for three of Peter Matthiessen's novels, which the famed author reworked into the National Book Award winner *Shadow Country*. And for good reason. First off, there seems to be something about gentleman killers that excites our interest—perhaps the odd juxtaposition of good manners and bad behavior. For another thing, the tale cuts a wide swath across the early twentieth-century South and West, from the Indian Territory (today's Oklahoma) to South Carolina, Arkansas, Texas and, of course, a chapter or two in Florida. Finally, Ed Watson is an early example of a serial killer: a man who appeared to take murdering a human being as lightly as killing a fly and did it considerably more often. In his lifetime, Watson is believed to have murdered, by stabbing or shooting, in the neighborhood of fifty men and women. Given his penchant for drowning his victims' bodies, though, we may never know for sure.

Quinn Bass. Sam Toland. Adolphus Santini. Belle Starr. Dutchy Melbourne. Hannah Smith. Lesly Cox.

Was the dapper man with the red hair and blue eyes thinking of any of his victims when he maneuvered his gasoline-powered launch toward the dock at Ted Smallwood's Store on Chokoloskee Island on October 24, 1910? Like most locals traveling through the Everglades, he knew Ted carried the supplies he needed. Why, the double-barreled shotgun in his hull was loaded with gunpowder he'd bought from Mamie Smallwood last time he'd stopped by.

As he drew the boat closer, the man looked in vain for his pal Ted among the crowd of twenty or so awaiting his approach. Instead, he saw angry faces, guns raised.

He tied down the boat and clambered up onto the dock.

"Who killed him?" one of them cried out. "Who killed Cox?"

"He fell into the water and drowned," he replied calmly. "What do you want with me?"

"Give it up, Watson," another man called. "You're finished."

He raised his gun, and they all raised theirs.

It was the moment Ed Watson had expected all his life.

Edgar J. Watson was born in Edgefield County, South Carolina, in 1855. His father was a violent prison warden known as "Ring-Eye" due to the knife scar encircling one eye. As a child, he and his mother, Minnie, lived in terror of his father and did everything they could not to raise his ire.

He was planting peas in the garden not long after his ninth birthday when a neighbor called out to him.

"Hey, boy! Where's your pa?"

"Dunno. At work, maybe."

The man moved toward him along the darkly furrowed earth.

"Better watch where you're throwing them peas, son," he said. "That's a mighty sloppy job you're doing."

The child felt his heart begin to race, but he didn't say a word. Reaching into his pocket, he scanned the horizon. Not a soul was in sight.

As the neighbor turned to leave, he suddenly fell forward into the dirt, stabbed by a rusty penknife in the back.

Afterward, Ed walked home for supper. His mother took one look at the knife sticking out of the pocket of her son's bloody overalls and began packing their bags. She didn't need to ask any questions. They caught the next train to Lake City, Florida, where she had family.

Ed's cousins taught him how to dress, how to speak well. But they were older and tended to lord it over him. He wanted to be a man, in charge, worthy of respect. So when he came of age, he married the first young girl who would take him. She was pregnant, so she couldn't easily afford to say no.

One night, Ed and his cousins got to playing darts in a neighborhood bar, and the drinking and ribbing got a little out of hand. He pulled out a .38 and shot one of his kin in the head. His other family members were too stunned to move, but three strangers went to grab him. On his way to the door, he shot them, too.

For the second time in his young life, Ed Watson was on the run. The next few years saw him making his way through Arkansas and Texas and way out to Indian Territory, sometimes in the company of outlaws like Belle and Max Starr. But the Bandit Queen, tough as she was, was sickened by the young man's cruelty. She told him she had half a mind to turn him in for some of the stunts he pulled during their jobs, some of the killing he'd done, just because he could. Not long afterward, she, too, was found dead, shot in the shoulder and the face, not three hundred feet from Watson's cabin.

Over the following years, Watson was accused of several more murders and assaults, sometimes over nothing more than being outbid at a land auction. Every time, his attorneys managed to get him off. They argued circumstantial evidence. Lack of credible witnesses. Reasonable doubt. He soon learned how to play the U.S. criminal justice system like a hand of poker.

And then, in 1892, it looked as though Ed Watson were at last going straight. He purchased Chatham Bend Key, one of the famed 10,000 Islands in the Everglades, for $250. Seventeen miles south of Chokoloskee, the forty-acre island was to be transformed, in less than two decades, into an agricultural empire. Watson became the most successful farmer in the Everglades, growing, processing and distributing everything from winter vegetables and sugar cane to syrup and buttonwood. He built a two-story frame house for his wife—his second—that aroused the envy of every visitor.

The odd thing was, his farmhands, mostly drifters from Punta Gorda and the Keys, kept disappearing. There was also word of his cutting the throat of a man named Adolphus Santini and paying $900 to settle the matter out of court. He didn't even know his victim Quinn Bass; he met him in a fight in an Arcadia tavern and broke it up with his Smith & Wesson. Then the man who didn't want to sell him Lostman's Key was discovered dead, along with his nephew. There were also Cox, and Smith, and Melbourne, all killed, apparently, at the same time. When a sheriff's deputy finally came calling to investigate some of these disappearances, Watson actually forced him, at gunpoint, to pick sugar cane and then return to the sheriff with a warning of his own.

It was Hannah Smith's corpse—so large that a leg was exposed in the water despite the weights placed inside—that sent the locals looking for other bodies in the vicinity. That's what led them to the showdown at Smallwood's Store.

On October 24, 1910, after a slight delay due to a disastrous hurricane, two dozen vigilantes waited for Ed Watson. He stepped out of the launch and raised his shotgun, but nothing happened—perhaps because the gunpowder was wet from the storm, perhaps because Mamie Smallwood had intentionally sold him a bad product. In any case, he could not fire.

The locals had no such problem. Thirty-three shots went off, and Ed Watson's killing spree was over.

## How Yeehaw Junction Got Its Name

As odd as the name "Yeehaw Junction" sounds for the rural intersection of U.S. Route 441/State Road 15, State Road 60 and Florida's Turnpike (Exit 193), it was once even stranger. Until the mid-1950s, the site, about thirty miles north of Lake Okeechobee and roughly the same distance west of Vero Beach, was known as Jackass Junction or Jackass Crossing, after the primary mode of transportation once used by local ranchers, cowboys and loggers to cross the unpaved terrain. Their destination: the town's main attraction, the Desert Inn and Restaurant, established in 1898 as a trading post and eventually converted into a gas station, bar, brothel and dance hall. The site was so important to the area that today it boasts a proud spot in the U.S. National Register of Historic Places.

When plans were made to run the turnpike smack dab through the town in 1957, state legislators decided a name upgrade was called for. And so the Osceola County community—population 240 as of 2010—borrowed

The Desert Inn at Yeehaw Junction. *State Archives of Florida/McDonald.*

its present name from nearby Yeehaw station on the Florida East Coast Railroad, a bit farther east. Which begs the question: where did the depot get *its* name?

It makes sense, as some claim, that travelers by mule would call out the southern expression of delight, "yee*haw*," on reaching the railroad depot. It also makes sense that the word is the local native (Creek, perhaps) word for "wolf" and has nothing whatsoever to do with happy cowboys.

In any case, it is believed that the ghost of a former owner of the Desert Inn still takes the time to rearrange the upstairs furniture or blast cold air down to unsuspecting guests, although that story, too, has its share of doubters. It may just be the spirit of an early disgruntled employee, also known now and then to toss a decorative mannequin across the dining room.

Yee*haw*!

# PART IV

# THE WIDE WORLD OF FLORIDA STORYTELLING

L ike Floridians in general, professional storytellers in the Sunshine State represent a variety of cultures. Unlike most Floridians, we perform our stories for audiences.

The vast majority of Floridians who know some of the folktales, legends and myths of their cultural heritage carry them with them much like they do any other part of their identity. They may sometimes draw them out for children or for a special occasion like a holiday observance. But otherwise, these stories exist in the back of their minds or in their hearts, consciously or otherwise. The tales may be the concrete manifestations of long-held values and beliefs. Or they may serve as cultural touchstones, remnants and reminders of who someone is and where his or her people came from. For the rest of us to understand and appreciate our neighbors, it helps to know some of their stories.

This section introduces important tales from many of the diverse groups living in Florida. It also includes thumbnail sketches of some of the important professional Florida storytellers who keep, or have kept, such stories and traditions alive.

## AFRICAN AMERICAN: UNCLE MONDAY, FLORIDA'S ALLIGATOR CONJURE MAN

African Americans arrived in Florida in the early nineteenth century, the vast majority of them refugees from the cruel yoke of slavery, just like the hero of the story below. They often mingled with the native tribes, finding refuge among members of another embattled community.

The great Florida folklorist, anthropologist and author Zora Neale Hurston collected a longer variant of this tale when she was doing fieldwork among African American communities for the Florida Federal Writers' Project in the 1930s. As is usually the case, multiple versions of the tale have been circulated. In fact, Monday is often called "Brother" instead of "Uncle," which is the familiar form of address for males in that community, from which the better-known "Brer" Rabbit gets his name.

The three great conflicts that occurred in Florida between the U.S. government and the Seminole people, known as the Seminole Wars, took place between 1817 and 1858. Lake Maitland, which appears in this story, is the largest lake in a town named for the fort built there in 1838, during the Second Seminole War.


Many years ago, at a time when the lines between human and nature, man and beast, were not yet drawn quite so firmly as they are today, there lived a great and good man named Uncle Monday. He was an African conjure man, also known as a root doctor, leaf doctor or *obeahman*, and he was a leader in the cult that was associated with the crocodile, one of the most terrifying of beasts. Whatever you chose to call his profession, Uncle Monday had mastered the ways of *hoodoo*, an important spiritual practice from his homeland that employed powerful spells and incantations, in addition to astonishing transformations.

Monday hadn't planned to ever leave the safety and comfort of his family. There was certainly plenty of need for hoodoo to keep him busy at home in his African village, and he was a respected figure there, with friends and admirers from far and wide. But like so many other proud Africans over the centuries, Monday was captured and sent to North America on a torturous journey aboard a slave ship. He was sold for a high price to a rich white master in the Carolinas. For the rest of his life, he would remember the violence, humiliation and horror of that experience. Maybe it was then that he began to plot his revenge.

Unlike many others in his position, Uncle Monday was fortunate to be able to escape his master. It was so dangerous for a slave on the run in those days that, quickly as he could, he made his way to Georgia and then on to Florida, where he hoped to blend in with the natives. Indeed, he and his new neighbors had much in common. At the time, the Seminoles were fighting their own bloody battles with the white man in order to remain in their homeland. The U.S. government, meanwhile, was doing everything it could to remove them, dead or alive.

"I believe I can help you," Monday told the chief. "I am not only a conjurer but also a warrior. I would like to throw in my lot with you against the conquerors."

It didn't take long for the chief to recognize the newcomer's skill. Monday proved himself to be a capable healer and a loyal friend. Most of all, the natives admired his energy. It was even said that they called him Monday because he approached every task with the energy and enthusiasm that most of us have only after a good, long Sunday off.

The natives fought bravely under Uncle Monday's leadership, but to no avail. After one terrible defeat, he led the drained and humiliated warriors to a heavily wooded area near the oval-shaped lake. They sat on the ground around the fire, expectantly awaiting his instructions.

When at last he spoke, Uncle Monday's voice was low and firm.

"I have consulted the gods," he said slowly, "and they have told me that we cannot overcome our enemies. Their weapons and their numbers are far superior. So I have decided what I will do. I will turn myself into an alligator—a cousin of my crocodile kin—and vanish into this lake until the day comes when men like us can once again walk this land in peace."

That night, it is said, the fire burned especially bright, and the tribe's chanting and drumming could be heard from miles around. At one point during the ceremonies, Uncle Monday began to dance. As the mesmerized men and women looked on, he danced faster and faster. Soon his skin grew thick and scaly, his arms and legs shortened, his jaw elongated drastically and his voice became a savage bellow. And then, when his transformation was complete, two rows of gators, a thousand strong, marched out of the lake to claim him as their leader. With a final look back at the warriors, he turned and led his new tribe back into the water.

## AFRO-CUBAN/LUCUMI/YORUBA:
## OCHOSI BECOMES AN ORISHA

Santeria, also known as Regla de Ocha or the Lucumi religion, is an African Diaspora belief system, born in Cuba, with roots among the Yoruba people of Nigeria and Benin. The name is related to the Spanish *santos*, or saints, which are known as the *orishas*. Each of these saints, or deities, corresponds to an aspect of human experience.

Santeria *patakis*, similar to myths, are considered a bridge between the spiritual and physical worlds. They explain how and why things came to be the way they are. Although variants of patakis often appear to contradict each other—for example, there is more than one account of the creation of humankind—the differences are of no concern to those who believe. That's because in Africa, each community had its own orishas and santos. Thus, in the New World, when people from multiple backgrounds came together as one group, the priests allowed the stories to coexist and complement one another. Such flexibility means that rather than being concerned with the literal truth of the stories, believers focus on what they teach about the human condition.

Today, practitioners of Santeria in Florida still leave *ebbós*, or ceremonial offerings, for the orishas whose assistance they require in any given situation. Animal carcasses regularly appear on the banks of the Miami River in supplication to the orisha Oshun, the river deity, who watches over sexuality, fertility, love and beauty.

If you were to show up on the steps of the Miami–Dade County Courthouse any weekday morning before the doors open, moreover, you may find burning candles; some sort of game (male goats, roosters, pigeons or quail); smoked fish or a rodent called a *jutia*; cigars; vegetables such as roasted sweet potato fries; and fruit, including pears, grapes, plantains, pomegranates, anisette and bananas. These are the favorite treats of the deity Ochosi, the supporter of those in trouble with the law, particularly if they are wrongfully accused. He is also a magician, fortuneteller, warrior, fisherman and, as you will see, hunter.

Long, long ago, when Ochosi was still as human as you or I, he was known throughout the land as an expert hunter who could always catch his prey with his trusty bow and arrows. One morning, he awoke earlier than usual, kissed his mother goodbye and went off to the woods to catch some supper for the family.

"I won't be here when you return," his mother called after him. "I am going to the market, and then I have some visiting to do after that. I will be back just in time to make our meal with whatever you've caught."

Later that day, Ochosi was in the midst of the forest when he came upon his friend Elegua.

"I am so glad to see you!" the warrior exclaimed. "Olofi is holding a party tonight in the heavens, and Orula wants someone to catch a rare bird so he can give it to him. I told him you were just the man for the job." Olofi is the divine ruler of the earth, and Orula is the orisha of wisdom and divination.

Glad to be of use to the orishas, Ochosi set out at once in search of the bird and, without much trouble, located and trapped it. He returned to his empty house, put it in a cage for safekeeping and set off to tell Orula what he had done.

Not long after he left, Ochosi's mother returned from the market. Her friend had not been at home, so she was back much earlier than she'd expected. When she saw the creature in the cage, she was very pleased.

"Ochosi is such a good boy," she said to herself. "This bird will make a wonderful meal for us." And with that, she killed the bird and prepared it for cooking.

Then she got to thinking. "Such a fine bird deserves some special spices." So off she went back to the market.

When Ochosi came home a second time and saw the dead animal, he was beside himself. What evil being could have killed Olofi's bird? How could someone behave so badly? Without a second thought, he went out to the forest and, thanks to his great skill, bagged a second bird in no time. This one he took immediately to Orula, who was overjoyed.

"Come with me to the party," Orula said, clapping the man on the back. "We can give this gift to Olofi together. I know he will be very pleased."

When the two ascended to the heavens and presented the bird to Olofi, the great orisha was delighted.

"To thank you for this deed," he said to Ochosi, "I give you this crown and proclaim you one of us. You, Ochosi, are now an orisha. I just haven't yet decided what your special task will be on earth."

The warrior was astonished at the unexpected honor. He bowed low in front of Olofi.

"You may rise," Olofi said. "Now tell me, is there something else I can do for you?"

Ochosi stood before the great Olofi and nodded. "Since you ask, yes, there is. This bird here is in fact the second I found for you today," he said. "The first was killed by someone who came into my home after I set it in a cage there. I would like to shoot an arrow and know that it will reach the heart of whichever evildoer took the life of that bird."

Olofi, who knew everything, knew who it was that had done the act, of course, and he knew what the killing of his own mother would do to Ochosi.

"Are you certain?" he asked. "After all, you have no idea who it is."

"Yes, I am," Ochosi said. "Whoever it was should not have killed what did not belong to him."

"All right then. Shoot your arrow, and it will find its mark."

As soon as the arrow flew forward from the bow, Ochosi heard a familiar cry. Rushing in the direction of the sound, his greatest fear was realized. His beloved mother was dead. He had shot her through the heart.

When Ochosi returned to the heavens to face Olofi, the assembled guests saw that his heart was broken. But he uttered not a word of remorse.

Impressed, Olofi addressed the newest orisha.

"I can see that you are horrified at your act. But at the same time you do not regret it, because justice needed to be served. I see that you will punish wrongdoing, no matter who is the perpetrator. From this day on, you will be a hunter of truth and a server of justice on earth."

And so it has been, to this very day.

## BAHAMIAN/JAMAICAN: ANANSI AND BROTHER DEATH

Depending on where and by whom his story is told, the Afro-Caribbean human/spider/god is known as Bosee Annansee, Ananse, Anansi, Aunt Nancy or just plain Nancy. Believed to originate with the Ashanti (or Asante) people in Ghana, Anansi stories traveled, beginning in the fifteenth century, via slave ships to the New World. At once a hero and a trickster, Anansi demonstrates to desperately oppressed peoples everywhere that brains can win out over brawn and that freedom is always worth fighting for. The following folktale, which probably began as a simple "how's come" or "*pourquoi*" story about why spiders weave their webs, is an example of how a seemingly simple tale can take on serious meaning when it is told at a time of great hardship and tragedy. Perhaps due to its theme of hope, it is one of the most important in both the Bahamas and Jamaica. In both countries, such stories were shared during old story time, once a time-honored family tradition. Here is one variant:

One day, Anansi was walking along a dusty country road when he felt that golden midday sun pouring down on his head and back like the sweetest of honey. He became so thirsty that he told himself he would stop at the first place he came to and ask for a drink. But he didn't see any houses anywhere.

He was nearly in despair when he spotted a small homestead with a nice, shady front porch and two rocking chairs. Sitting on one of them was a skinny old man, dressed all in black, with not an ounce of flesh on his bones and even less hair on his head.

"Excuse me, sir," Anansi said, in his most pleasant voice. "I sure would like a glass of water, if it isn't too much trouble."

The man didn't say a word.

Anansi cleared his throat. "I *mean*, sir, could I have a drink of water?"

Still the old man kept silent.

Anansi shrugged, brushed past the homeowner and through the front door and helped himself to a drink. Then he turned around, and to his delight, he saw a beautiful table groaning with goodies: rice and peas and fried plantains, jerk chicken and curried goat, conch fritters and cabbage and just about anything he might possibly want to eat. Once his thirst was taken care of, he realized how hungry he was. So he sat himself down and helped himself.

When he had eaten and drunk his fill, Anansi walked out the front door and patted the old man on the shoulder.

"Why thank you kindly, sir," he said. "What's that you say? Come back tomorrow? Why, thank you! Don't mind if I do!"

And every day for a week, the spider returned to the house for a hearty meal.

But on the eighth day, Anansi got to thinking. Sometimes the way the chicken was spiced was not exactly to his liking. And his daughter's conch fritters could, quite frankly, run rings around the old man's.

So he returned with his daughter, a fine young girl of marriageable age.

"I'd like to offer my daughter's hand in marriage, sir," he said, taking the girl by the arm and leading her over to the old man. "If you'll agree, I know she'll make you a good cook. I mean *wife*."

The old man nodded in agreement. Never one to skip a meal, Anansi proceeded inside and helped himself to the spread.

"This is good," he said to himself, "but the old man's food is going to get much, much better."

Then he went on his way, promising to return the next day.

When he returned, however, he didn't see his daughter, just her clothes piled neatly on a chair.

"Where's my girl?" he asked the man.

The old man rubbed his belly as if to say, "In here. I ate her."

Anansi almost fainted. Only now did he know the identity of the silent old man. He was, in fact, Brother Death. Anansi had to get out of there quick!

But before he could take a step, the old man jumped up and started to chase Anansi. He chased him out of the house, down the road, into the town and all the way back to Anansi's own home.

"Quick!" Anansi screamed to his family as he ran through the door. "Jump on the ceiling so Brother Death can't get at you!"

Up on the ceiling, the spiders wove elaborate webs so they could hold on up there for a long time. It was a good strategy, and it worked, for a while. But it just wasn't possible to hold onto a web forever. First his wife and then each of his remaining six children dropped from the ceiling into the burlap bag Death had set out for them in the middle of the floor.

Finally, only Anansi himself, grief-stricken and terrified, was left on the ceiling. That's when he hit on a plan.

"Excuse me, Brother Death," he said. "I have eaten so much of your food that my body is as heavy and brittle as a big glass ball. I'm afraid that if I fall, I will shatter, and then I won't be of any use to you or anyone."

Death stared up at him, listening.

"But if you were to roll a barrel of flour underneath where I'm hanging, I can fall into it, and all will be well."

Death did exactly as Anansi suggested. And when Anansi let go of the ceiling and fell, he reached out for Death's face and pushed it deep into the barrel of flour. It didn't keep Death down long. But it gave Anansi and his family time to run away. And so Death had to wait to catch them another day.

## CRACKER: THE EDUCATION OF EPAMINONDAS

As with any good traditional tale, this one has been set in cultures as diverse as Afghanistan and the American West. It is a perennial, perhaps, because everywhere we go we meet someone sillier than we ever thought possible. Or is it just me?

In southern folk narratives, the grandiose name that has stuck to this foolish character (if you don't count the famous Jack, who shows up throughout Appalachian tales) makes the story all the funnier. To make matters even better, in none of the variants I've seen have I found a nickname for the main character. The real Epaminondas, or at least the one who actually existed, was a true hero: a general and statesman of Thebes in ancient Greece. Born about 2,400 years ago, he seems to have borne little resemblance to the protagonist of this lovely little tale, a Cracker favorite. Although it's fun to think that he resembled him as a child.


Epaminondas was a good boy; everybody said so. He'd do whatever his mama or granny told him to do. All he wanted was to be helpful.

One day, Epaminondas was playing in the yard when his mama called him over.

"Epaminondas, child, come here a minute. I want you to wash your hands and take this here cake I've baked over to your granny. And whatever you do, mind you don't drop it! She's expecting to serve it for supper tonight."

Well, the little boy was careful. He was sooo careful, in fact, that he hugged that gooey cake to him all the way over to his granny's. When he got there, the old lady took one look at the boy, another look at the cake, another look at the boy, another look at the cake, and she shook her head.

"Lordy, you are the darnedest fool child I've ever seen! The next time your mother gives you something like that, hold it on your head so it don't get crushed! You got that?"

"Yes, ma'am."

Well, you sure didn't have to tell Epaminondas nothing twice. About a week later, his mama gave him a big hunk of butter, freshly churned.

"Take this straight to your granny," she said. "Remember, no lollygagging!"

Well, Epaminondas wanted to do the right thing. All he wanted was to be helpful. So he remembered what his granny had said the last time, and he put that old hunk of butter on his head.

By the time he arrived to his granny's house in that harsh Florida heat, the butter had melted clear down past the vicinity of his ears and onto his neck. His granny took one look at the boy, another look at the butter, another look at the boy, another look at the butter, and she shook her head.

"Lordy, you are the darnedest fool child I've ever seen! The next time your mother gives you something like that, take some cabbage leaves down to the stream, chill them in the water, then wrap them around it until it's very cold, then carry it carefully in your hands. You got that?"

"Yes, ma'am."

Well, you didn't have to tell Epaminondas nothing twice. About a week later, his mama said, "Child, I want you to bring one of these new puppies over to your granny to keep her company. She's been asking for one for ever so long now."

Well, Epaminondas wanted to do the right thing. All he wanted was to be helpful. So he remembered what his granny had said the last time, and he took some cabbage leaves down to the stream, and he chilled them and chilled them, then he wrapped them around the puppy until it was very cool, and then he carried it carefully in his hands.

At least he tried to. By the time he got to Granny's, the puppy was clear on the other side of town.

His granny took one look at the boy, and one look at the cabbage leaves, then another look at the boy, and another look at the cabbage leaves, and she shook her head.

"Lordy, you are the darnedest fool child I've ever seen! The next time your mama gives you something like that, tie a rope around it and lead it on over here. You got that?"

"Yes, ma'am."

Well, you sure didn't have to tell Epaminondas nothing twice. About a week later, his mama gave him a loaf of freshly baked bread to take over to his granny.

"Now get it to her while it's still hot!" she said. "I don't want you taking no detours!"

Well, Epaminondas wanted to do the right thing. All he wanted was to be helpful. So he remembered what his granny had said the last time, and he tied a rope around the bread and led it over to her house.

By the time he got to Granny's, the bread that remained tied with rope was dirty and ragged and nothing anybody would want.

His granny took one look at the boy, then another look at the boy, then a third look at the boy, and she shook her head.

"Lordy, you are the darnedest fool child I've ever seen!" And that was all she said.

The next week, Epaminondas's mama baked six sweet cherry pies. She carried them out the front door and put one on each step to cool.

"Child," she said, calling him from the yard. "I will bring a pie over to Granny's myself when I go out. As for you, young man, when you come in and out of this house, mind the pies! Be careful where you step!"

Well, Epaminondas wanted to do the right thing. All he wanted was to be helpful. So the very next time he climbed the stairs, he was careful to step smack dab in the center of each pie.

And that is the last anyone heard of Epaminondas.

## CUBAN: THE BOSSY GALLITO

It is no overstatement to say that the decade and a half following the 1959 Cuban Revolution changed the face of Miami forever—and the 1980 Mariel boatlift only exacerbated that change. Today, as many as 1.4 million Cubans make their homes in Florida, the vast majority of them in Miami, with an estimated 400,000 of them having arrived after 1980. The second-largest concentration of Florida Cubans, an estimated 80,000, live in the Tampa/ Ybor City area.

Miami-based storyteller and librarian Lucia Gonzalez learned the following story from her aunt when she was a child back in Cuba. She has published a picture book under the same name. Here is my retelling, with her permission:

There was once a *gallito*, a little rooster, that just had to have his own way. There was no nice way to say it: the fowl was bossy.

One day, the bossy gallito was invited to his uncle's wedding. He cleaned his feathers, combed his comb and set out on his way. But as luck would have it, the rooster was soon stopped in his tracks by his very favorite delicacy in the whole wide world: three kernels of golden corn. He would have gobbled them up without a thought, except for the fact that the corn was nestled in a muddy patch of road. And if his beak were to get muddy, how would he go to his uncle's wedding?

Ah, he thought, there will be plenty to eat at the wedding.

Then he thought: But will they have corn?

Then he thought: But I don't want to be late.

Then he thought: But I didn't have breakfast!

Then he thought: But I don't want to get dirty.

Then he thought: But I can wash myself off!

And so he convinced himself that he could eat the corn. One, two, three, he gobbled up all three golden kernels. Delicious!

There was just one problem: his beak was filthy.

He continued on his way until he came upon a patch of grass.

"Hey you there, grass!" he called in his bossy way. "Come over here and wipe my beak so that I can go to my uncle's wedding!"

Well, the grass was none too happy to be spoken to that way, so he said, "No, I won't!"

The gallito was angry, but he continued on his way. It was then that he saw a goat.

The Bossy Gallito was only polite to his friend the Sun. *USDA.*

"Hey you there, goat!" he called again in his bossy way. "Come over here and eat this grass, because it won't wipe my beak, so I can't go to my uncle's wedding!"

Well, the goat was none too happy to be spoken to that way, so she said, "No, I won't!"

The gallito was steaming mad, but he continued on his way, only to find a stick.

"Hey you there, stick!" he called again in his bossy way. "Come over here and beat this goat, because it won't eat this grass, because it won't wipe my beak, so I can't go to my uncle's wedding!"

Well, the stick was none too happy to be spoken to that way, so he said, "No, I won't!"

The gallito was furious, but he continued on his way, until he saw a small fire smoldering in the brush.

"Hey there, fire!" he called again in his bossy way. "Come over here and burn this stick, because it won't beat that goat, because it won't eat that grass, because it won't wipe my beak, so I can't go to my uncle's wedding."

Well, the fire was none too happy to be spoken to that way, so she said, "No, I won't!"

The gallito was livid, but he continued on his way. Soon he came to a babbling brook.

"Hey you there, brook!" he called again in his bossy way. "Come douse this fire, because it won't burn this stick, because it won't beat that goat, because it won't eat the grass, because it won't wipe my beak, so I can't go to my uncle's wedding!"

Well, the brook was none too happy to be spoken to that way, so she said, "No, I won't!"

The gallito was beyond furious. Just then he saw his good friend the sun.

"Sun, my dear friend!" he said in a friendly way. "I'm so glad to see you! Will you please dry up that brook? Because it won't douse that fire, because it won't burn that stick, because it won't beat that goat, because it won't eat that grass, because it won't wipe my beak, so I can't go to my uncle's wedding!"

It's nice to be talked to that way, isn't it? So the sun said, "Of course, my friend! My pleasure!"

Well, when the brook heard that, she said, "Okay, okay! I'll douse that fire!"

When the fire heard that, she said, "Okay, okay! I'll burn that stick!"

When the stick heard that, he said, "Okay, okay! I'll beat that goat!"

When the goat heard that, she said, "Okay, okay! I'll eat that grass!"

When the grass heard that, he said, "Okay, okay! I'll wipe your beak! Now you can go to your uncle's wedding!"

And so he did.

## HAITIAN: TEZIN NAN DLO

Kric? Krac! That's the traditional call-and-response opening to a Haitian story told live, which to this day often takes place after the sun is down, the supper dishes are washed and family members young and old have gathered on the porch to let their imaginations run wild.

The Haitian population in the United States stood at about five thousand in 1960; but with the ending of the Duvalier government in the late 1980s, immigration from this close Caribbean neighbor increased. Today, the U.S. Haitians number well over half a million, with about half of them residing in Florida, mostly on the southeast and southwest coasts.

Two of the most famous characters in Haitian folk narrative are Bouki the Trickster and Malis, his foil. In story after story, they get into scrapes that reflect, usually in a good-natured way, the greed and selfishness of humankind.

The equally popular tale of Tezin, which I retell below, is more serious, based as it is on the voodoo understanding of human encounters with nonhuman beings. It is a type of tale called a *kont chante*, or song tale, because it is told with a few lines of melody that are repeated throughout. (For most western storytellers, the term is *cante fable*, which means the same thing in French.)

In Haitian Creole, the name *Tezin* means, literally, "hooked," and it is a lovely metaphor for the joys and challenges of adolescence. *Nan dlo*, incidentally, means "under the water."

When a girl approaches the age of marriage, the time at which she will soon leave her family house and set up a home of her own, her parents may become unusually protective. They want her to marry well, and they want her to remain pure until she does so. They know, better than she, that the world can be a cruel and dangerous place.

At least that is what one particular mother and father felt to be true about their own beloved daughter, whom, as she grew into a young woman, they watched with equal parts pride and dread.

Their daughter was a good child, already grown into a fine young lady. Among this young lady's household tasks, it fell to her to fill two buckets of water every day from the nearby river and carry them back to the house. She prided herself on bringing back the clearest water of any of the young women in the village. In truth, if anyone were to ask her, she couldn't have explained how she had managed to become so skillful. She just knew that wherever she placed her buckets, they would attract the best water, as if by magic.

Then one day, as the girl dipped her buckets into the flowing river as usual, a giant fish jumped out on the shore as if to greet her. At first she drew away from it, terrified at its size. But as she looked more closely, she realized it was surely the most beautiful fish she had ever seen, with dazzling silver fins and warm, sensitive brown eyes.

And then, to her shock, it spoke to her, in a voice as gracious and delightful as befit the owner of those eyes.

"Young woman," the fish said, "I have watched you collect water here for many years. You are always so cheerful and so kind to the other females. And you are always so careful not to hurt any of my brother fish. You are indeed unique among your species."

The girl was so surprised to hear the fish talk that she was speechless at first, but then she nodded and said, "Thank you. I always try to do my best."

"I would like to be your friend," the fish continued. "My name is Tezin. Whenever you need me, or want the freshest water, or anything at all, you just have to call me with this little song:

*Tezin of the waters, Tezin, friend from the waters*
*Tezin of the waters, Tezin, friend from the waters*
*Tezin, my true friend*

*Tezin nan dlo bon zanmi mwen Tezin nan dlo*
*Tezin nan dlo bon zanmi mwen Tezin nan dlo*
*Tezin bon zanmi mwen.*

The fish didn't tell the young girl to keep their meeting a secret, but somehow she knew that she should. And so when she returned home that day with her buckets of water, she didn't say a word about her strange encounter, either to her parents or her brothers.

But you know when you have a happy secret, how hard it is to keep it from those who know you well? The girl moved around the house that evening as though she were dancing inches above the floor. At first no one paid her any attention, so busy was the family with the ordinary duties of life.

But as time went by, the girl would rush to take her buckets down to the river first thing in the morning. She would stand by the shore, singing:

*Tezin of the waters, Tezin, friend from the waters*
*Tezin of the waters, Tezin, friend from the waters*
*Tezin, my true friend*

*Tezin nan dlo bon zanmi mwen Tezin nan dlo*
*Tezin nan dlo bon zanmi mwen Tezin nan dlo*
*Tezin bon zanmi mwen.*

Maybe in the beginning she rushed because she was so grateful for the clear, clean water. Maybe later it was because she enjoyed the big fish's company. But before very long, the girl had fallen deeply and completely and joyfully and miraculously in love with the big fish Tezin. It was written in the creases of happiness around her mouth and in the sparkle of her eyes, in the rhythm of her footsteps and in the lightness of her voice.

Her mother and father at last noticed the change in their daughter, and they did not like it. They knew something was different, something they could not control, something that threatened their child and their family. To them, it smelled like voodoo, the strongest of witchcraft, which had somehow taken hold of their sweet girl.

The parents talked about what they should do. They decided to send their youngest boy to follow his sister to the river and see what, or who, was behind her great happiness.

"A girl isn't happy like that without something or someone to make her that way," they told each other. "We need to be sure that she is protected."

By this time, the girl was fairly racing to the river and warbling her song on the way. Her brother, who struggled to catch up with her, took careful note of the words, the tune and the giant fish that emerged when she sang. He also saw that the fish and the girl held each other tightly and danced together to a different melody, one that appeared to be audible to only the two of them.

"Our time together is not long," the fish whispered to her as they danced. "You will know I am gone when you see three drops of blood on your breast."

The girl was alarmed, but the fish was so close to her, and she was so happy, that she put the warning out of her mind as quickly as it had come.

Later that evening, when the little boy told his parents what he had seen and heard, they knew there was only one thing for it.

"This is the devil," they told each other. "We must take care of our daughter."

"Daughter," they called. She came at once; she was an obedient child.

"Daughter, we want you to go to the market tomorrow. One of your brothers will carry the water."

She nodded and said nothing, but in her heart she was no longer quite as joyful, because she knew she would not see her beloved Tezin.

The next day, when the girl was away at the market, the parents took a long spear to the river. Then the mother sang the song in her daughter's voice:

*Tezin of the waters, Tezin, friend from the waters*
*Tezin of the waters, Tezin, friend from the waters*
*Tezin, my true friend*

*Tezin nan dlo bon zanmi mwen Tezin nan dlo*
*Tezin nan dlo bon zanmi mwen Tezin nan dlo*
*Tezin bon zanmi mwen.*

Up jumped the big fish out of the water and onto the shore, only to be stabbed, repeatedly, by the girl's father. Then he threw Tezin back into the river until he sank, lifeless, to the very bottom.

At that moment, in the market, the girl felt an odd wetness on her breast. She looked down at her blouse and counted one, two, three drops of blood. Without completing her shopping, she walked back home in dread, as though her pockets were filled with bricks.

The moment she arrived in the house, she smelled the lunch cooking.

"Come to the table, children!" her mother cried. "We've got fresh fish, and lots of it!"

"I am not so hungry today, mother," the girl said, her eyes filling with tears. "I would like to lie down, if I may."

When they looked in on her later, all they saw was the top of her chair and a few hairs from her head. And then they wept, too. There was nothing they could do after all to protect their dear girl. She had disappeared underground to become one with her beloved.

## JAPANESE: AMATERASU THE SUN GODDESS

Amaterasu is one of the most important characters in both Shinto and Japanese mythology. One of the most prominent reflections of the small but important Japanese presence in Florida is the Morikami Museum and Japanese Gardens in Delray Beach, built by George Sukeji Morikami. Morikami was one of the last remaining members of the group that established the agricultural settlement known as the Yamato Colony in south Palm Beach County in 1905, so named by founder Jo Sakai because it was the ancient word for Japan.

Amaterasu was the firstborn child of the creator god Izanagi and his wife, Izanami. She was born from her father's left eye, when he cleansed it after purifying himself following a visit in the underworld.

When the young girl came of age, her parents, who were very powerful, gave her a jeweled necklace. They also made her goddess of the sun, which gave her mastery over the sky. Beautiful and powerful, Amaterasu made the sun rise every morning, bringing joy and growth to the earth.

Amaterasu had two brothers, one named Tsukuyomi and the other named Susano-o, as well as a sister called Waka-hiru-me. While Tsukuyomi ruled the heavens with his sister for a time, Susano-o was the storm god, ruler of the sea plain. And to be sure, storms followed the mischievous god wherever he went.

Apart from her regular duties as sun goddess, Amaterasu taught humans how to weave cloth and plant rice. One afternoon, the two sisters were quietly weaving together in the weavers' hall when there was a loud crash. Something big and heavy had fallen through the roof. The sisters ran to see what it was. To their horror, it was a skinned horse. And through the hole in the roof, they saw the laughing Susano-o.

The sun goddess's beautiful face blazed red, but she didn't say a word.

Not long afterward, Amaterasu caught her little brother destroying rice fields.

"Susano-o!" she cried. "This is unacceptable! These fields belong to the humans who planted them, not to you!"

But again Susano-o just laughed.

Then came the day the sun goddess found her brother spreading filth throughout her sacred temples. And that, as they say, was the last straw.

"I'll show you!" Amaterasu screamed. "I'll show you all what happens when you anger the sun goddess!" And with that, she disappeared into a cave in the heavens and sealed the entrance.

At first no one noticed. The sun was setting anyway, and Amaterasu never showed herself at night. But the next morning, when the cocks crowed to greet the morning sun, she didn't appear.

"Amaterasu Oho-hiru-me!" the people called. "Oho-hir-me-no-muchi! Where are you? Why are you sleeping so late?"

But the goddess would not answer.

Soon the people were frantic. "The rice won't grow without you, Amaterasu!" some called out.

"You have plunged us into total darkness!" others howled. "Evil spirits are wandering the earth! You must come out and save us!"

The other gods and goddesses knew they had to do something to get her out, and fast. They placed roosters outside the sealed entrance, in the hopes that the crowing would inspire her to appear from force of habit, but it was no use. Then they brought out a large sakaki tree, decorated with all manner of shiny jewels, luxurious white dresses and a full-sized mirror. When a young goddess began a lewd dance in front of it, the others, despite their concern, laughed in response.

Amaterasu was still angry, but she was also curious. She had to find out what was causing them to enjoy themselves so much without her! When she stepped out just to take a quick look, she froze. Who was that stunning goddess standing there before her?

Not until after one of the strongest gods had grabbed her did she realize her error. It was only her own reflection in the mirror that had caught her attention.

"Let me go!" she yelled. "You cannot do this!"

Amaterasu fought with all her strength to return to the cave, but by then other gods had barred the entrance. And so she returned to the sky, where she remains to this day, bathing all creation in her heavenly light.

## JEWISH: ELIJAH WORKS IN MYSTERIOUS WAYS

Although Jews arrived in Florida as early as 1763—and possibly accompanied Ponce de Leon as *conversos*, or hidden Jews, in 1513—by the time statehood was declared in 1845, not even one hundred were in evidence. Things started to change, however, with the first Jewish institution, the Jacksonville Hebrew Cemetery, created in 1857. By the turn of the century, the state boasted six Jewish congregations.

By 1928, the Jewish population had grown to 10,000, the majority of whom were still in Jacksonville. Today, the state's Jewish population is closer to 750,000, many from the Caribbean and South and Central America, and many of these have settled in South Florida.

Perhaps the most beloved prophet of the Jewish people is Elijah, who is said to regularly make his presence known throughout history. Even today, each spring, when families celebrate the freeing of the Hebrew slaves from Egypt at the Passover Seder, they open the door to welcome their old friend and protector. He is also said to assist the Torah (Bible) scholar working on a thorny problem, and he performs miracles for families in distress. Perhaps most importantly, he is believed to be present at the *b'rit milah* (ceremonial circumcision), when the eight-day-old Jewish male enters into a covenant with God.

This is a story about some of Elijah's miracles—and how he, like God, often employs methods and reasoning that are mysterious to human understanding.

Many years ago, a simple tailor was making his way across a lonely road on a winter evening when he came upon an old, white-bearded man in a white caftan. He knew, without quite knowing how he knew, that he was face to face with the great prophet Elijah, and he could barely control his excitement.

"Excuse me, please, Elijah, sir," he said, approaching the older man. "It is such an honor to meet you. I wonder if you could answer a question I have long puzzled over."

"Walk with me," Elijah replied. "And I will do what I can for you."

Falling into step with the prophet, the tailor said, "I was wondering if you could, if you could explain…" Here his voice faltered a bit.

"Do not be afraid, young man," the prophet said kindly. "What is it you wish to know?"

"I was wondering if you could explain to me why it seems as though—excuse me, but it seems that time and time again, the righteous suffer, while good things come to those who are selfish and greedy and unkind."

The prophet walked on silently for a while. Then he said, "The best way for me to answer that question is to invite you to accompany me on my journey. But I must insist that you promise not to say a word about my methods."

The tailor's heart soared with joy. At last, he would understand one of the deepest problems of the universe!

"I promise," he said solemnly. "I will not utter a word."

As they walked, the sun was setting, and the temperature dropped. Before long, the pair reached a poor, miserable street. They stopped at the most wretched shack, really just a few warped boards held together by several rusty nails. Elijah knocked on the door, and in a few moments, a grizzled, bent old man opened it.

"We are travelers passing through," said Elijah. "May we impose on you for the night?"

The old man stepped back to welcome them in. "Our home is yours," he said. "The best of what we have we offer to you with pleasure."

Well, the best of what the old man and his wife had to share were a few sad-looking potatoes for supper and a bug-infested lump of a bed for sleep. The poor couple themselves spent the night on a straw pallet on the ground.

When the travelers awoke in the morning, they found the woman of the house weeping.

"What is the matter?" the tailor whispered to his host.

"Our cow died during the night," he answered with a frown. "We don't know how we will make a living without her."

When Elijah and the tailor left the home, the young man turned to the prophet.

"You see, this is what I was wondering," he said. "These are such nice people. Why would—?"

"You promised not to speak," Elijah replied. "Just wait. All shall be revealed."

The two men walked on until they reached a wealthy home with a glass roof that seemed to float in the sky and enormous doors of the finest cedar. The sun was setting, and the Sabbath, the holiest day of the week, was just beginning.

A servant responded to Elijah's knock. When the prophet explained that they were travelers and asked if they could share a Sabbath meal and spend the night, the servant said, "I must ask my master."

In time, he returned to the door and directed them around to the back of the house. There he let them in, bade them sit on the floor of the kitchen and gave them scraps from the master's table.

The pair slept that night in the stable. While they lay among the animals and the hay, a horrendous storm blew down from the heavens, with winds that seemed to shake the very earth.

In the morning, the servant sent them on their way without a scrap to eat. As they passed out the back door, the tailor noticed that a mighty oak alongside the house had nearly been ripped from its roots by the storm. At that moment, workmen were carefully stabilizing it so it wouldn't destroy the structure.

The tailor turned to Elijah. "The wealthy master of this house gave us nothing," he said. "Why was his home protected from the storm?"

"You promised not to speak," Elijah replied. "Just wait. All shall be revealed."

The two soon arrived at the luxurious synagogue of the rich man's community. The seats were swathed in velvet, and every man was dressed in the richest gabardine. But not a word of welcome was spoken to the strangers.

After the service, Elijah stood at the vast double doors of the building and addressed the crowd. "May every one of you emerge a great leader," he said. Then the two went on their way.

"I just don't understand," the tailor said after walking several minutes in silence. "Those men didn't say a word to us. They have everything they could possibly want except kindness. Why would you—?"

"You promised not to speak," Elijah replied. "Just wait. All shall be revealed."

The two men had come nearly full circle in their wanderings. Their next stop was the poor man's house of worship, so small that those who prayed inside had nowhere to sit. Still the crowd made room for the two strangers, handing them their own prayerbooks and prayer shawls and bidding them welcome.

At the end of the service, Elijah stood at the narrow front door and blessed the crowd. "May one of you emerge to be a great leader," he said.

As they took their leave, the tailor nearly exploded in frustration.

"I don't understand at all!" he cried. "These men were so kind, and yet you blessed them with just *one* great leader, while to the others you promised a roomful of them! How is that just?"

At last Elijah turned to the tailor. With a sigh, he took hold of the man's shoulders.

"All right," he said. "I will explain. You remember that old couple we stayed with? God had decreed that the woman should die that very night. The sorrow would have killed her husband for sure. I begged him to simply take the cow, which will be replaced."

"I see," the tailor said. "That does make sense. But the rich house? Why was it spared damage from the storm?"

"A treasure beyond value is buried at the roots of that tree," Elijah said. "Had it collapsed all the way over and destroyed the house, the owner would have found himself rich as a sultan."

"I see," said the tailor. "That does make sense. But why did you bless the wealthy *shul* [synagogue] and curse the poor one?"

"I did no such thing," Elijah replied. "Who wants many leaders in a community? That is indeed a curse. The poor community will have one leader. That is my most precious blessing."

At last the young man was speechless. And so the two parted company, with the tailor understanding just a little bit more about Elijah's mysterious ways.


## NICARAGUAN: LA MOCUANA

Whether they came to the United States to escape the Sandinistas in the late 1970s or to flee poverty at any other time, Nicaraguan immigrants and their families today number close to 400,000, with about 30 percent of these living in Miami–Dade County alone. Largely based on the sixteenth-century Spanish conquest and the influence of their patriarchal, Catholic culture, Nicaraguan folk narratives tend to center on two overarching themes: the treachery of the Spanish conquerors and the dangers often posed by mysterious women. For example, one popular legend, "La Carretanagua" (the Naqua Cart), is based on the pulling of ox carts through the streets, on which the Spanish piled either plundered gold or dead peasants.

Often the two elements of Spanish conquerors and wronged women occur in the same story. "La Cartaginesa" (the Woman from Cartago), "La Llorona" (the Weeping Woman), "La Segua" and "La Mocuana," the last of which may be based on true events, are variants on the theme of women betrayed by Spaniards—who, in turn, terrorize unsuspecting Nicaraguan men.

A good-sized hill stands on the east side of the highway at La Trinidad, Esteli, a two-hour ride due north from Managua and not far from the mountains of Matagalpa. It is called La Mocuana, in honor of a poor Indian princess who lost her way.

This princess was the light of her father's eyes. The *cacique*, or chief, entrusted his daughter with many of the secrets of his reign. She proved to be a worthy confidante and adviser, blessed with wisdom and patience. Beyond that, she was quite beautiful, with a long neck, delicate shoulders and rich, shiny black hair that rippled down her back like the finest of silk.

One day, the chief learned from a neighboring tribe that the Spanish conquistador Rojas was in the area. He knew that the Spaniards craved gold above all things, even more than women and slaves.

"My dear," he said to his daughter that evening, as he poured out some small nuggets of gold from a leather bag onto a cloth. "We will treat the Spaniards like honored guests. It is the only way we can retain our dignity and, perhaps, our lives."

La Mocuana nodded and reached for one of the pieces. She held it up, and it shimmered in the firelight. "I hope this is enough for them," she said. "I hope they will take these shiny pieces and leave us alone."

It wasn't long before the conquerors reached the tiny village. The tallest and broadest of them, dressed in his hard helmet and armor, strode over to the chief, who invited him to sit and join him in a meal. Then the chief handed him the gold.

The Spaniard, who had been sour-faced and somber up to that point, broke out into a grin. He spoke very fast and nodded many times. At the end of the meal, the cacique stood up, thanked him for coming and sent him and his men on their way. The surprised Spaniards simply did what they were told and went the way they had come.

Father and daughter congratulated themselves on their cleverness.

"But we must not be naïve," said the chief. "Did you see how that big man's eyes gleamed at the sight of gold? We must hide what we have left, in case they come back looking for it." The two buried the rest of their treasure deep in the earth by a certain hill so they would have no trouble locating it again when the time was right. They swore to tell no one what they had done.

The following night, the Spanish soldiers returned to attack the village, their swords and lances drawn. The brave warriors of the cacique retaliated, and the fight raged on for quite some time. When it was over, the few remaining Spaniards retreated, bloody and humiliated.

Father and daughter congratulated themselves yet again, this time on the bravery of their fighters. The gold was still untouched.

Many months went by, and it appeared as though the Spanish warriors had passed over that part of the country. But then one day, the princess, who was used to wandering well past the village, came upon a handsome, bearded young Spaniard. He was not wearing armor, only simple clothing, almost like those of a peasant. He looked small. He looked lonely.

She could not say why she didn't hide and return home to tell her father at once. It was something in the way he was so alone. She wondered if he were lost.

Cautiously, she approached him. In her language, she said, "I am the princess of my people. Who are you? What are you doing here? Where are your friends?"

The young man spoke for some time, but all she understood were his soft tones and his dark eyes.

She thought: "He is so different from the men of my village."

She thought: "I have never touched a beard before."

After that first meeting, the two came together nearly every day, and though they learned only a few words of each other's language, she began to feel she knew his deepest thoughts.

"A good man," she told herself. "Not like the others. A gentle soul."

Of course, her rendezvous had to be kept secret. But the villagers began whispering and asking questions. Worse still, her father began talking to her of finding a mate.

One night, when she had stayed so late with the Spaniard that she had no idea what she would say on her return, she came to a decision. Next time, she would not leave him. But she had to show him a way forward. She had to prove, to herself as well as to him, that they would be all right.

They had been sitting by the fire; now she reached for his hand and pulled him to his feet. Slowly, she led him to the hill. Her heart pounding, she dug into the soft earth until she reached the rest of her father's gold nuggets, bigger and brighter than anything he had handed over to the Spaniards. She held them up for him to see. Then, in her best mixture of languages and pantomime, she told him her plan. To run away. To be together.

He looked at the gold and smiled and nodded. Then he held her in his arms and looked at the gold once more.

The next evening, when she went to find the Spaniard at his hut, bringing with her the few possessions she had, he was gone. Shaking with fear, she made her way to the hill. The gold was gone, as well.

She fell onto her knees, raised her face to the sky and felt the tears streaming down her face like water from a bowl. Just then, a blanket was thrown over her face and body. Someone was tying it around her. Screaming and kicking, she found herself deposited—where?

She knew it was a mountain cave by the dark and fierce cold that enveloped her. As she struggled to release the ties, she heard someone seal the opening with heavy rocks and dirt. She had no doubt then that the plan was to kill her.

But the princess was nothing if not resourceful. Using small, sharp rocks, she was able to carve an opening out of the other side of the cave. The work was so long and tedious, and she cried so hard, that by the time she emerged into the fresh air she had nothing to smile about. Her fingers were ragged and bloody, her eyes were wild and she had nowhere to go. She knew that her village would not accept her back. If she were in her father's place, she would not do so, either.

It is said that to this day, La Mocuana wanders the countryside at night, tearing out her hair in misery, in search of men to destroy, particularly drunks and playboys. It is said that her village's gold is buried deep in the hillside near Matagalpa.

## SEMINOLE: THE ORIGIN OF THE CLANS

Native Americans have populated the land we now know as Florida for thirteen thousand years or more. It is estimated that prior to European arrival in the sixteenth century, the Timucua, Apalachee, Ais, Jeaga, Tekesta (or Tequesta), Calusa, Pensacola, Tocobaga, Matecumbe, Mayaimi, Ocale, Potano and Guale peoples in the area numbered 100,000 or more. They flourished, proving successful trappers, hunters, fishermen and farmers.

As in other regions of the United States, the next centuries brought disease, slavery, war and resettlement to natives throughout the Southeast. By the 1770s, Creeks (who included the Miccosukee) from Georgia and Alabama had moved south to escape their own troubles with settlers. They merged with the Florida survivors to form a new tribe, the Seminoles, meaning "wild people" or "runaways." They were joined by other natives, as well as runaway African slaves.

By the end of the 1800s, the Seminole population had dwindled to just three hundred. Thanks in large part to their familiarity with the Everglades, the unfamiliar landscape of which stymied U.S. troops, they were never defeated. Today, Florida's "Unconquered People," as they call themselves, number about two thousand. They live mainly in reservations in Big Cypress, Brighton, Fort Pierce, Hollywood, Immokalee and Tampa.

The Seminoles are perhaps best known to outsiders for their involvement with casinos and tobacco. But their age-old connection to the natural world is so strong that a creation story that Seminole storyteller Pedro Zepeda considers central to the culture does not involve human beings at all. Due to the tribe's diverse roots, its traditional stories feature characters and plot elements that may at times contradict one another. But most important of all are the values underlying the tales.


The Creator is known by many names. Breath-maker. Hisagita Misa. Grandfather. From his home in the Milky Way, he fashioned the animals. He made horses and cows and dogs and birds, reptiles and insects and fish and many others. From time to time, he would touch certain animals longer than others, giving them special powers, including the power to heal.

Among all his creations, the Panther—Coo-wah-chobee—was the Creator's favorite. He liked the feel of its sleek fur as he petted it. He liked the way it moved, slinking so smoothly and surely and close to the ground.

Seminoles on Big Cypress Reservation. *Library of Congress.*

He liked its strength and patience. There was something majestic about the creature. Excellent qualities in an animal, he thought, more than once.

So it was that when the Creator decided to create the earth for the animals to populate, he took Panther aside.

"Panther," he said, "it is no secret that you are my favorite among all the creatures. When the earth is finished, I want you to be the first to set foot upon it. You are special."

At long last, the earth was complete. The Creator gathered all the animals together and placed them in a giant shell, which he set among the tallest mountains.

"Just wait a while," he told them. "Soon this shell will split, and you will be able to take your rightful places on the earth. Some of you will go out to the jungles, some to the deserts, others to the swamps, the oceans or the air. You will see for yourselves where it is that you belong." Then he sealed the shell shut.

As time went by, the roots of a nearby tree began to grow around and around and around the shell. Many moons came and went. Alongside the shell stood a great tree. As time passed, the tree grew so large that its roots started encircling the shell. Eventually, a root cracked the shell. The Panther was patient, which the Creator usually admired. But in this particular situation, Panther was just a bit too patient. The Wind started circling around the crack in the shell, round and round the inside edges, so vigorously that the crack grew ever larger.

The Wind remembered that the Creator wished for the Panther to be the first creature outside of the shell. "We will fulfill the Creator's wishes," he said, reaching down to help the Panther take its rightful place on earth.

The Wind was everywhere. The Wind, after all, is the air we breathe. After the Wind helped the Panther out first, the Panther thanked him for the honor. Next to crawl out was the Bird. The Bird had picked and picked around the hole and, when the time was right, stepped outside the shell. Bird took flight immediately. After that, other animals emerged, each at its own pace. Bear. Deer. Snake. Frog. Otter. There were thousands of creatures, so many that no one apart from the Creator could even begin to count them all. All went out to seek their proper places on earth.

Meanwhile, as Bird was flying around looking for a spot to live on earth, the Creator was watching. He watched each animal and did not intervene, preferring to leave the animals on their own. The Creator often allows things to happen in their own time. The Creator wanted a thing to occur on its own merits.

When the Creator saw that all was done, he decided to name the animals and put them into clans. For being such a good companion, the Creator rewarded the Panther's clan with special qualities: "Your clan will have knowledge for making laws and for making the medicine that heals," the Creator told Panther. "You, the Panther, will be in possession of all the knowledge of these different things. The Panther will have the power to heal many different ailments, as well as to enhance a creature's mental powers."

The Creator believed that the actions of the Wind were honorable and noble as well, so he told the Wind, "You will serve all living things so they may breathe. Without the Wind or the air, all will die."

"The Bird, for being able to take flight, will be the ruler of the earth," continued the Creator. "The Bird will make certain that all things are put in their proper places."

So this is how the beginning came to be. Some call it the Creation. Though there were many, many animals put on this earth by the Creator, all came to know their proper places upon it.

## THE WIDE WORLD OF FLORIDA STORYTELLERS

Florida's professional storytellers keep the oral narrative tradition alive, whether they are sharing traditional, literary or personal tales on stages, in classrooms and libraries or at festivals. If only I could include them all! Instead, here is a small sampling of Florida storytellers past and present whose work reflect their unique culture and vision.

The story of the Florida Storytelling Association (flstory.com), meanwhile, goes back to the early 1980s, when storytellers Jennifer Bausman and Annette Bruce decided to celebrate the U.S. storytelling revival in their home state. The result: the first Florida Storytelling Camp in 1984, featuring renowned performers. The festival was embraced, in 2000, by a brand-new statewide membership organization, the Florida Storytelling Association. Now the camp has morphed into the Florida Storytelling Festival, which takes place at the end of each March in Mount Dora. The two-hundred-plus-member organization supports and educates storytellers and story enthusiasts looking for professional support, engaging entertainment and like-minded community.

### Roslyn Bresnick-Perry (1922–2015)

Roslyn Bresnick-Perry was born in a tiny village called Wisockie-Litewsk in present-day Belarus. For years a "snowbird" in Deerfield Beach, Perry spent the rest of her time in New York City. She earned a National Storytelling Network Lifetime Achievement Award for her tales of Jewish life in "the old county" and senior life in the new, most of which appear in the award-winning book *I Loved My Mother on Saturdays and Other Tales from the Shtetl and Beyond*.

### Annette J. Bruce (1918–2011)

Annette Jenks Bruce was a native of Eustis. An author and storyteller, she founded the first Florida Storytelling Camp in 1984, which led to the creation in 2000 of the Florida Storytelling Association. Her numerous publications include *Cracker Tales* and *Sandspun: Florida Tales by Florida Tellers*, with fellow Florida storyteller J. Stephen Brooks.

## Lucille Francis-Fuller (1937–2014)

Lucille Elorine Francis-Fuller, affectionately known as "Mummy," was born in Portland, Jamaica. Apart from her work as a TV host and producer, philanthropist, certified nurse's assistant, bookseller, educator and counselor, she was a master storyteller for the Florida Department of State Bureau of Florida Folklife Programs Division of Historical Resources.

## Lucia Gonzalez

Born in Calmito del Guayabal, Cuba, Lucia Gonzalez is an award-winning storyteller, author and children's librarian based in Miami-Dade County. Her bilingual books include *The Bossy Gallito* (El Gallo de Bodas), *The Storyteller's Candle* (La Velita de los Cuentos) and *Señor Cat's Romance*. Among her many honors, she received the Jean Key Gates Distinguished Alumni Award from the University of South Florida School of Library and Information Science.

## Tamara Green

Tampa-based, Memphis-born Tamara Green was the Florida Storytelling Association's Youthful Voices director. She is an acclaimed storyteller and adult and youth workshop presenter whose love of stories comes from her father, Willie Frank Glover, a master storyteller whose tales centered on life in the Mississippi Delta. Along with African, African American and Florida tales, she tells what she calls "citified urban tales."

## Butch Harrison

Butch Harrison has entertained groups in the Live Oak area and beyond Suwannee County with his authentic Cracker tales. Most of his repertoire comes from his own life experience around the ocean, the Florida Keys and the Everglades—a life spent handling cattle and horses, catching alligators, fishing, gigging frogs and serving as an airboat operator and guide in the Glades.

## Betty Mae Jumper (1923–2011)

Born Betty Mae Tiger (Potackee) in a Seminole camp near Indiantown, Jumper was herself a Seminole legend. The only female chief of the Seminole tribe of Florida, she was also a nurse, newspaper editor and writer; the 1997 Florida Commission on the Status of Women Woman of the Year; and the author of the collection *Legends of the Seminoles*.

## Liliane Nérette Louis

Since the 1980s, Liliane Nérette Louis has told the tales of her Haitian culture at festivals, schools and libraries. She served twice as a master artist in the Florida Folklife Apprenticeship Program and twice won the Florida Individual Artist Fellowship in Folk Arts. Her book *When Night Falls, Kric! Krak! Haitian Folktales* appeared in 1999. Louis offers Haitian cooking courses and is well versed in the use of plants in Haitian culture.

## Lucrece Louisdhon-Louinis

South Florida storyteller Lucrece Louisdhon-Lounis is also a dancer, former librarian and library administrator and current executive director of the Louines Louinis Dance Theater Inc. Her Haitian and Caribbean-themed performances earned her and her husband, Louines, the prestigious 2016 Florida Folk Heritage Award.

## Bob Patterson

Storyteller, singer, songwriter and guitar player Bob Patterson co-founded the Gamble Rogers Folk Festival and has been its artistic director for twenty-one years. The award-winning musician has recorded eight albums and published two books of Florida history and folklore. A former board member of the Florida Storytelling Association, Bob received its Lifetime Achievement Award.

## Virginia Rivers (1935–2003)

Raised in Ybor City, teller Virginia Rivers was a teacher, educational TV host, children's librarian and puppeteer. She co-founded the Florida Suncoast Puppet Guild and the Tampa Bay Storytellers Guild. She also served three decades as artistic director of Creative Arts Theater for the City of Tampa and was known as the guiding light of the Tampa–Hillsborough County Storytelling Festival. Her daughter Kim, who has chaired the Florida Storytelling Association, carries on the family tradition.

## Gamble Rogers (1937–1991)

A musician as well as storyteller, Gamble Rogers is perhaps best remembered for his stories of fictional "Oklawaha" County. His tales featured characters such as Agamemnon Abramowitz Jones, Downwind Dave and Sheriff Hutto. Throughout the 1970s, Rogers was a favorite at the Florida Folk Festival, and he was inducted after his untimely death into the Florida Artists Hall of Fame.

## Linda Spitzer

Linda Spitzer is a native Floridian storyteller with a master's degree in storytelling from East Tennessee State University. A puppeteer and magician, she was the Storylady for ten years at the historic Biltmore Hotel in Coral Gables and directed and produced storytelling programs on Miami cable TV. Her extensive oeuvre includes a wealth of Jewish folktales.

## Kuniko Yamamoto

A native of Osaka, Japan, storyteller, mime and origami artist Kuniko Yamamoto studied dance, music and theater. She learned mime from famed teacher Tony Montanaro, has performed with the Leland Faulkner Light Theater and has appeared at such prestigious venues as the National Storytelling Festival, the Kennedy Center and Epcot.

## *Pedro Zepeda*

Pedro Zepeda is an artist, woodcarver and Seminole cultural interpreter born and raised in Naples, Florida. Zepeda graduated from Stetson University with a degree in fine arts. It was at the Seminole tribe's Ah-tah-thi-ki museum that he honed his skills in traditional arts and interpretation of his culture. Zepeda learned traditional Seminole stories from his grandmother and other tribal elders.

# SELECTED SOURCES

Austin, Daniel F., and David M. McJunkin. "The Legends of Boca Ratones." *The Spanish River Papers* (Boca Raton Historical Society) 9, no. 3 (May 1981).

Bennett, Jim. "Bone Mizell: Cracker Cowboy of the Palmetto Prairies." *Wild West*, October 1999. www.historynet.com/bone-mizell-cracker-cowboy-of-the-palmetto-prairies.htm.

Bruce, Annette. *Tellable Cracker Tales*. Sarasota, FL: Pineapple Press, 1996.

Bruce, Annette J., and J. Stephen Brooks. *Sandspun: Florida Tales by Florida Tellers*. Sarasota, FL: Pineapple Press, 2001.

Bucuvalas, Tina, ed. *The Florida Folklife Reader*. Jackson: University Press of Mississippi, 2012.

Bucuvalas, Tina, Peggy Bugler and Stetson Kennedy, eds. *South Florida Folklife*. Jackson: University Press of Mississippi, 1994.

Burt, Al. *The Tropic of Cracker*. Gainesville: University Press of Florida, 1999.

Carlson, Charlie. *Weird Florida: Your Travel Guide to Florida's Local Legends and Best Kept Secrets*. New York: Sterling House, 2005.

Carr, Patrick. *Sunshine States: Wild Times and Extraordinary Lives in the Land of Gators, Guns, and Grapefruit*. Gainesville: University Press of Florida (Florida Sand Dollar Book), 1999.

Congdon, Kristin. *Uncle Monday and Other Florida Tales*. Jackson: University Press of Mississippi, 2001.

Elder, John L. *Everlasting Fire: Cowokoci's Legacy in the Seminole Struggle Against Western Expansion*. Edmond, OK: Medicine Wheel Press, 2004.

Glassman, Steve, ed. *Florida in the Popular Imagination. Essays on the Cultural Landscape of the Sunshine State.* Jefferson, NC: McFarland, 2009.

Goss, James P. *Pop Culture Florida.* Sarasota, FL: Pineapple Press, 2000.

Hall, Lynne L. *Strange but True Florida.* N.p.: Sweetwater Press, 2005.

Jay I. Kislak Foundation, Inc. *Myths and Dreams: Exploring the Cultural Legacies of Florida and the Caribbean.* Exhibition Guide. Miami Lakes, FL: J.I. Kislak Foundation, 2000.

Kelly, Doug. *Florida's Fishing Legends and Pioneers.* Gainesville: University Press of Florida, 2011.

Kleinberg, Eliot. *Weird Florida.* Cocoa Beach: Florida Historical Society Press (Chapin House), 2006.

———. *Weird Florida II: In a State of Shock.* Cocoa Beach: Florida Historical Society Press (Chapin House), 2006.

Klinkenberg, Jeff. *Pilgrim in the Land of Alligators.* Gainesville: University Press of Florida, 2008.

Lapham, Dave. *Ghosts of St. Augustine.* Sarasota, FL: Pineapple Press, 1997.

Louis, Liliane Nerette. *When Night Falls, Kric! Krac! Haitian Folktales.* Edited by Fred Hay. Englewood, CO: Libraries Unlimited, 1999.

Martin, C. Lee. *Florida Ghosts and Pirates: Jacksonville, Fernandina, Amelia Island, St. Augustine, Daytona.* Atlglen, PA: Schiffer, 2008.

McIver, Stuart B. *Dreams, Schemers and Scalawags: The Florida Chronicles.* Vol. 1. Sarasota, FL: Pineapple Press, 1994.

———. *Glimpses of South Florida History.* Miami: Florida Flair, 1988.

———. *Murder in the Tropics: The Florida Chronicles.* Vol. 2. Sarasota, FL: Pineapple Press, 1995.

Patterson, Bob. *Forgotten Tales of Florida.* Charleston, SC: The History Press, 2009.

Reaver, J. Russell, ed. *Florida Folktales.* Gainesville: University Press of Florida, 1987.

Shine, T.M. "Your 1994 St. Valentine's Day." *Sun-Sentinel,* February 13, 1994. articles.sun-sentinel.com/1994-02-13/lifestyle/9402100651_1_al-capone-valentine-s-day-massacre-alibi.

Sloan, David L. *Ghosts of Key West.* Key West, FL: Phantom Press, 1998.

Wippler, Migene Gonzalez. *Legends of Santeria.* Woodbury, MN: Llewllyn, 1994.

## Selected Websites

www.americanfolklore.net
www.anansistories.com
www.bellamybridge.org
www.bermuda-attractions.com
www.bocahistory.org
www.exploresouthernhistory.com
www.flstory.com
www.hauntedhouses.com
www.hauntedplaces.org
www.history.org
www.mylakeokeechobee.com
www.naplesnews.com
www.nicaragua-guide.com
www.roadsideamerica.com
www.robertthedoll.org
www.semitribe.com
www.skunkape.biz
www.smithsonianmag.com
www.tcpalm.com
www.urbanlegendsofsouthflorida.com
www.ussugar.com
www.voodoomuse.org
www.weirdus.com

# ABOUT THE AUTHOR

Caren Schnur Neile, PhD, is a performance storyteller and affiliate professor at Florida Atlantic University, where she has taught storytelling studies since 2001. Dr. Neile has performed and lectured throughout the United States and abroad, including as a Fulbright Senior Specialist in universities in Jerusalem and Vienna. She is the former chair of the National Storytelling Network and is a former co-founding editor of the international academic journal *Storytelling, Self, Society*. Dr. Neile co-hosts *The Public Storyteller*, a weekly segment on South Florida public radio WLRN 91.3 FM. Her numerous publications include the book *The Great American Story*, and she contributes a regular column on storytelling for the *Florida Jewish Journal*.